WHATEVER HAPPENED TO BRITAIN?

D1136533

WHATEVER HAPPENED TO BRITAIN?

The economics of decline

John Eatwell

Duckworth

British Broadcasting Corporation

Published to accompany a series of programmes in consultation
with the BBC Continuing Education Advisory Council

© 1982 John Eatwell
Third impression September 1983
Second impression December 1982
First published April 1982

Published by the British Broadcasting Corporation
35 Marylebone High Street, London W1M 4AA
and Gerald Duckworth and Co Ltd
43 Gloucester Crescent, London NW1

ISBN 0 563 16545 6 (cased) (BBC)
ISBN 0 563 16544 8 (paper) (BBC)

ISBN 0 7156 1643 9 (cased) (Duckworth)
ISBN 0 7156 1639 0 (paper) (Duckworth)

Photoset in North Wales by
Derek Doyle & Associates, Mold, Clwyd,
printed in Great Britain by
Redwood Burn Ltd., Trowbridge, Wiltshire, and
bound by Pegasus Bookbinding, Melksham, Wiltshire

Contents

Preface

This book was conceived in sorrow and in anger: sorrow over the meanness and misery that is infecting so much of economic life in the United Kingdom, and anger, not only that nothing significant is being done about it, but also that economics is failing to provide any coherent answers to what is, in many respects, an economic problem. Inveighing against economists may seem rather unfair. They are, after all, only the intellectual standard-bearers of far more important political forces. But the economists are responsible: with their ideas they have connived in the diminution of Britain. I decided therefore to relate events and ideas in an attempt to illustrate the way Britain's economic and intellectual history has contributed to her current plight.

A book such as this will inevitably be seen as advocating 'a programme', whether as a panacea or a miracle-cure; and any programme necessarily involves political intent. My own political prejudices will be clear to the reader, but I have tried to restrain them as far as possible, for I am convinced that the economic propositions I outline are not as politically controversial in general as they are in the British context. Those who disagree with the argument should, therefore, confront it on its economic merits, and recognise the fetters which history has placed on Britain.

The book was written in association with a BBC television series of the same title. The idea and inspiration for the project came from Robert Albury, to whom I am extremely grateful. I have been aided and abetted by a large number of BBC staff, notably Tony Roberts, the producer of the series, Colleen Lewis, Peter Maniura and Nick Metcalfe. I picked up some useful points from Niall Kennedy and Dave Jewitt.

The economic ideas developed here have been greatly influenced by – indeed, borrowed from – my Cambridge colleagues, particularly Nicholas Kaldor, Joan Robinson, Bob Rowthorn, Ajit Singh, Roger Tarling and Frank Wilkinson. I am confident that they will not be entirely happy with what I have done with their ideas; I hope they will believe that it was all in a good cause. I have received help and advice from Vladimir Brailovsky, Diane Flaherty, Chris Gregory, Roy Green, Alan Hughes, Prue Kerr, Hélène Seppain and Isabelle Weiss. I am grateful also to Murray Milgate, from whom I have learnt so much over the past few years, and to Emily Wilkinson, who provided important editorial advice. The staff of Duckworth amazed and entertained me by their speed and efficiency throughout the production process – a mere two months from receipt of copy to finished books.

Trinity College, Cambridge   J.E.
January, 1982

I

Independent of Men's Will

Britain's economic plight is far worse than that of other Western countries. The depression is destroying not only Britain's economic well-being, but also the quality of life – even life itself. The traditional villains – big unions, big companies and big government – cannot be blamed for Britain's decline. All of them defer to the market. The market system controls production and distribution and is the ultimate arbiter of economic success. Economics was developed in an attempt to understand how the market works. This understanding is necessary for any interpretation of what has happened to Britain.

*   *   *

Being British isn't as much fun as it used to be. In the first two decades after the war, when Britain's decline in the world was accompanied by full employment, the new family car, the comfort of 'never having had it so good' and the Beatles, her dismal economic performance could be shrugged off with that air of self-deprecation the British have long cultivated at home to match the air of effortless superiority they adopt abroad. But when that decline is manifest in three million unemployed, in the transformation of industrial estates into industrial wastelands, in the reduction of social services that have come to be taken for granted, and, worst of all, in an ominous feeling that there is no end in sight, self-deprecation gives way to anxiety and cynicism, and the facade of effortless superiority becomes distinctly tatty.

What has gone wrong? There is a predictable cast of villains to take the blame, and popular support can always be gained for specific explanations. Industrial disputes, inefficient management, workers' indolence, excessive taxation, incompetent and wrong-headed government, an effete ruling class, the Common Market – the list is virtually endless. It is much more difficult to present a persuasive general argument which will explain these various factors (in so far as any of them have substance) and sort the symptoms from the disease. Moreover general solutions tend to be merely apocalyptic – when what we want is some indication of what should be done.

This book does not offer a 'solution', nor indeed a detailed list of things to be done, but the final chapter does summarise the issues that must be faced in any recovery programme. These issues emerge from the history of Britain's current plight and from an examination of the various economic ideas that have from time to time captured the imagination of politicians and businessmen and so influenced economic policy. For in the forming of modern Britain ideas have been as important as events.

Indeed the current political debate over the fate of Britain is a debate about ideas – about different interpretations of how the economy works, of why it is going wrong and of what should be done about it. To understand where the country stands, therefore, and how it got there, we must understand the ideas that economists and politicians have about the workings of the economic system, and why they think the way they do.

But whether we are dealing with facts or theories, it will be a long view. I shall not be concerned with the problems and policies of the present government or its immediate predecessors. Instead, my purpose is to stand back and ask the questions: How did Britain get into this mess? How can we understand what is happening? What, if any, are the fundamental laws of behaviour that guide the operations of the economy?

The decline of Britain

After the end of the Second World War the West enjoyed a period of prosperity which was quite unparalleled. The early post-war years were fairly difficult everywhere. Queues, shortages and rationing

Table 1. Growth rates of gross domestic product, gross domestic product per head of population, and manufacturing output per person hour, 1950-1980 (percentages)

Gross domestic product

	UK	US	W. Germany	France	Italy	Japan
1950-60	2.6	3.2	7.6	4.4	5.9	8.1[a]
1960-70	2.5	3.8	4.1	5.6	5.5	11.1
1970-80	1.8	2.8	2.8	3.7	4.0	5.3

Gross domestic product per head of population

	UK	US	W. Germany	France	Italy	Japan
1950-60	2.2	1.6	6.5	3.5	5.3	7.0[a]
1960-70	2.2	2.6	3.3	5.0	4.7	10.0
1970-80	1.8	1.7	2.7	3.6	3.2	4.0

Manufacturing output per person hour

	UK	US	W. Germany	France	Italy	Japan
1950-60	2.3[b]	2.0[b]	5.9[b]	3.6[b]	4.1[b]	n.a.
1960-70	2.9[c]	4.0[c]	5.7[c]	6.8[c]	6.6[c]	12.1[c]
1970-80	2.9	2.4	3.9	4.8	4.5	6.4

Notes (a) = 1953-1960
(b) = total output (sum of all sectors) per person hour
(c) = 1963-1970
n.a. = not available

Sources:
A. Maddison, *Economic Growth in the West*
OECD *National Accounts*
OECD *Industrial Production*
National Institute Economic Review

Gross domestic product is the sum of all goods and services produced in a country. Gross domestic product per head of population is, therefore, the amount of goods and services 'available' to each citizen. Output per person hour measures the productivity of labour employed.

were the norm throughout Europe. But in almost all major countries unprecedented rates of growth were soon achieved, which transformed the lives of almost everyone with a flood of consumer goods. Yesterday's Hollywood fantasies no longer looked quite so fanciful. Even Britain grew faster than she had ever grown before in her industrial history.

But in the last ten years success has turned sour, and the nagging doubts and anxieties of the pre-war Depression, once apparently banished for ever, have returned in new and disturbing guise. Was the post-war prosperity a flash in the pan? Can the Western system still provide the material basis for the improving standard of living that all have come to expect – indeed to need? Or is the Western system, after running a new, brilliant course, now falling back exhausted into the 1930s – when the only viable solutions for economic ills seemed to be the military ones?

Nowhere is this questioning more urgent than in Britain. The Western system may be doing badly, but Britain is doing significantly worse than the rest. Indeed Britain did significantly worse during the whole golden post-war era. The prosperity enjoyed then masked an insidious deterioration in Britain's relative economic power. There is only one notable exception in the catalogue of foreign success, the United States – the only major Western economy which has experienced growth rates of output per head and industrial productivity as low as those in Britain. The land of free enterprise and business schools and no significant welfare state has seen its relative position in the world economic stakes decline almost as rapidly as the U.K.'s.

Of course the United States began its decline from a much higher level! And in the last ten years, though output per worker has grown as little as in Britain, total manufactured output at least has risen by nearly 40 per cent – as it has in Canada, France and Italy. In Japan it has risen by 56 per cent. In Britain it was an incredible three per cent *lower* in 1980 than in 1970. *Three per cent lower.* So in the last ten years Britain has had no companion in failure. She stands alone.

Britain's decline has been a decline in manufacturing industry more than anything else. While her manufacturing output fell, her gross domestic product – a term which encompasses the output of all goods and services from agriculture, manufacturing and oil to banking, entertainment and the services of the corner shop – rose by 20 per cent in the seventies. (By contrast gross domestic product rose by about 32 per cent in the United States and West Germany, by 45

Table 2. Gross domestic product and output in manufacturing industry 1960-1980. Indexes 1970 = 100.

Gross domestic product

	UK	US	W. Germany	France	Italy	Japan
1960	76.1	68.5	63.2	58.2	58.4	34.8
1970	100	100	100	100	100	100
1980	120	132	132	144	148	168

Manufacturing output

	UK	US	W. Germany	France	Italy	Japan
1960	75.6	61.9	55.8	54.9	49.7	26.1
1970	100	100	100	100	100	100
1980	97	137	123	135	138	156

Sources: OECD *National Accounts*
OECD *Industrial Production*

per cent in Canada, France and Italy, and by 70 per cent in Japan.) In the two years 1979-81, 1.6 million jobs disappeared in Britain, and 80 per cent of the jobs lost were lost in manufacturing. The country that was once the workshop of the world is now in the grip of *de-industrialisation*: a process in which the waning strength of her manufacturing is relentlessly ground down by superior competitors.

Economic decline and the quality of life

But does it really matter, it may be asked. Manufacturing is not the most pleasant of pastimes, and economics isn't everything after all. Surely in many intangible ways Britain offers a quality of life which is the envy of the world. The pageantry of royalty, the elegance of Henley, Wimbledon and Ascot, the unarmed police, the cosy pubs, the civility of everyday communication – all these are part of a way of life which seems to transcend economic decline.

There is a darker side to the story, however. Fewer houses are being built, so that in the long run housing is deteriorating. Mental health statistics showed a considerable worsening in the 1970s. In 1978 the citizens of England and Wales were two-fifths more likely to be convicted of drunkenness than they were in 1960 and nearly twice as likely to be in prison as in 1955.

All these trends indicate a general *decline* in the quality of life – indeed a decline in life itself.   social trends

The relationship between recession and mortality is now firmly established. International comparisons are difficult, and death rates are affected by many factors; but the conclusion is inescapable that

Figure 1

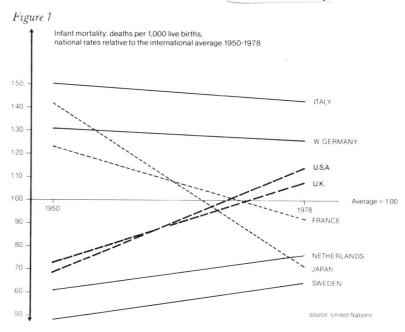

Infant mortality: deaths per 1,000 live births, national rates relative to the international average 1950-1978

Infant mortality measures the number of babies who are born alive but die in the first year of life. This number has fallen steadily since the war in all the countries of our sample, as a result of advances in medical care and the improvement in the general level of material well-being. The average number of deaths per thousand live births in our sample countries fell from 42.3 in 1950 to 12.3 in 1978. The diagram shows the relationship between national rates of infant mortality and this average. As standards become more uniform, all rates would be expected to move towards the mean. What we find, however, is that while West Germany, Italy, the Netherlands and Sweden have all improved at or near the average rate, with some tendency towards the mean, France and Japan, the fastest-growing countries, have achieved impressive gains and the slowest-growing countries, the United Kingdom and the United States, have suffered a severe deterioration. Indeed the deterioration in these two countries has been so great as to carry their rate of infant mortality from below to above the mean.

unemployment kills. For every extra million unemployed in Britain, there will be about 10,000 extra deaths every year, significantly more than the number of people killed in motor accidents.

Moreover Britain's slow rate of economic growth, relatively to her major partners in the West, has meant that the relative health of her population has tended to decline. This is best shown in the figures for infant mortality. The number of babies who die in the first year of life is affected by nutrition, health care, housing, education, clothing and so on – all the things that make up anyone's definition of the quality of life. After the war, the development of the National Health Service and the rapid advances made in medical science led to a dramatic fall in the rate of infant mortality, though the rate in Britain has never been as low as in Scandinavia or the Netherlands. But since 1955, while infant mortality has continued to fall in absolute terms, there has been an inexorable rise in comparison with other industrial countries. Gains in medical science and standards of nutrition have made relatively less impact in Britain than in France or Japan. Again the United States is Britain's only rival in this dismal trend. Italy and West Germany, who have always had depressingly high rates, have at least not seen a general relative increase.

The quality of life, defined in terms not of garden parties or pageantry, but of food, clothing and infant survival of the first year of life, is closely related to the rate of economic growth. Unless Britain's growth rate at least recovers, the comparative post-war deterioration in living standards will become an absolute decline.

Some traditional explanations

Why is this happening to Britain? Britain, after all, was the country which more or less invented the modern industrial age. Though there may have been costs, surely some advantages must accrue to the inventor of the game? Britain is politically stable – with a skilled, sophisticated labour force, a flexible, imaginative financial system, a high general level of education and enormous reserves of oil, gas and (most important of all) coal. All the ingredients for economic success are present in abundance. If Britain were a company, she would be a striking example of unrealised commercial potential – ripe for a takeover!

An immediate, and comforting, reaction is to look for someone to pin the blame on. The three customary villains are *big unions, big companies* and *big government.*

Trade unions

Though it takes two to quarrel, the trade unions are often blamed for the bad state of industrial relations in Britain. In turn the bad state of industrial relations is seen as the key element in Britain's relatively poor economic performance.

Strikes are the most obvious disruptive action in which unions are involved, and Britain certainly has a good many strikes. But compared with other countries whose economies have fared much better than hers, Britain is not particularly strike-prone. From 1969 to 1978, for example, there were on average 2,701 stoppages per year as a result of industrial disputes, while in the same period in Japan there were 2,694. In Britain the average number of workers involved in each stoppage was 484. In Japan it was 643. Japanese strikes, however, did not last as long as British strikes, averaging $2\frac{1}{2}$ days as against the British 8. In both cases we should remember that the number of days lost through strikes was minute, and certainly less than the number lost through illness. Or, to put it another way, the days lost in strikes each year are equal to three days' idleness endured by Britain's three million unemployed.

There is some relationship between strikes and economic performance – the more successful countries losing fewer days' work through strikes – though it is not very strong. Italy, for example, which through the sixties and seventies was one of the fastest-growing Western economies, has the worst strike record of all. But even within such a relationship, in so far as it exists, what is cause and what is effect? It can be argued, as indeed I shall argue, that Britain's poor economic performance has *caused* poor industrial relations as much as vice versa.

Big companies

What then of the big companies? Britain, to a far greater degree than her competitors is dominated by large firms with world-wide interests. Foreign-owned multinationals account for a large proportion of British industrial capacity, with a concentration of foreign ownership in 'strategic' manufacturing sectors, such as motor-cars and electronics.

Companies are in business to make profits, wherever they may be found, and cannot afford to be patriotic. As Adam Smith put it in his *Wealth of Nations* (1776):

> The proprietor of stock is properly a citizen of the world, and is not necessarily attached to any particular country.

Following this dictum, British companies have indeed invested heavily abroad. But foreign companies have also invested heavily here. In fact, foreign firms have invested more in Britain since the war than British firms have invested abroad, and they have tended to improve Britain's overall economic performance by being more efficient than domestic firms. Moreover the economies of other countries, such as Germany and Italy, which have performed far better than Britain, are also dominated by large companies, many of which are foreign. Japan, by contrast, has very few foreign companies, though Japanese industry is ruled by the great industrial combines, the *zaibatsu*. Indeed all research indicates that, as far as general economic performance is concerned, there is not much difference between large firms and small firms. All in all, while industrial companies large and small are principal actors in industrial investment and production, and can bring distinctive qualities to the performance of their roles, they seem to have only a limited influence on the overall direction of the play.

Government

That leaves big government. Can the relatively poor performance of the British economy be attributed to the heavy burden of unproductive and wasteful government activity that weighs down industry and stifles initiative? Are high taxation and excessive expenditure the real culprits?

In 1978 tax revenue and social security contributions totalled 34 per cent of Britain's gross national product. In Sweden they totalled 54 per cent, in France 38 per cent and in West Germany 40 per cent. Even in the slow-growing United States they were 31 per cent. Britain is *under*taxed in comparison with her industrial rivals.

In the same year in Britain government expenditure was 37 per cent of the national product. In Sweden it was 58 per cent, in France

42 per cent and in West Germany 41 per cent. In the United States it was 31 per cent. The British government therefore is an *under*spender as compared with its rivals.

Perhaps, then, it is the welfare state which is sapping Britain's competitive drive? If so, she can look forward to better days, since her competitors must be weakening more rapidly. For while Britain spent 17 per cent of gross national product on education, health and welfare in the mid-1970s, the Netherlands spent 29 per cent, Sweden 22 per cent and France and West Germany 21 per cent. Only the United States spent less than Britain, at 16 per cent. In comparison with her industrial competitors, Britain *under*spent on welfare.

Indeed, with the notable exception of Japan, where the spending role of the state is comparatively small, those countries which have been most successful in terms of economic growth are also those in which the state commands the largest share of national product. Again, whether this be cause or effect could be argued either way; but it would be difficult to argue that high levels of state activity diminish economic performance.

'Events' take control

All in all, it is hard to pin the blame on the traditional villains. Trade unions, companies and governments are, of course, the main agents of all economic activity. Any given level of performance must therefore have something to do with all three. But the attempt to blame any of them exclusively, or to blame all of them together, would be misleading – not least because no single one could be claimed to be 'in control' of the economy. Fundamentally they react to events, they don't determine them.

This obeisance to events on the part of the major institutional agents in the economy is seen most clearly when one of them is forced to behave in some way which will prove unpopular with its own constituency. If no scapegoat is immediately available, then 'reality', 'the world situation', 'the crisis', 'the recession', 'the state of trade' and generally 'events beyond our control' are presented as vindication. Trade unions, large companies and governments readily agree that they do not fully control economic events. If trade unions were in control, they would secure jobs and rising real incomes for their members. If big companies were in control, they would avoid the profits squeeze and bankruptcy. If governments were in control, they wouldn't risk being thrown out of office as a result of economic failure. All governments agree that they have been tossed around by the 'world system'.

The market system

What then is this 'system' to which trade union leaders, corporate executives and governments all defer?

The fundamental characteristic of economic life in the West is the market. Western nations may have many differences of history, national custom or institutional structure, but they are all 'market economies'. Whether the market is modified or restricted, manipulated or neglected, it *is* the system. Whether it be the world market, the capital market, the money market or the labour market, economic activity in the West is organised through, and responds to, the market.

Of course markets of one sort or another have always existed. In fact they must necessarily exist in any society which is not composed of self-sufficient isolated individuals. But the role that markets play in economic life – indeed even the social significance of the act of exchange – can vary from one system of social organisation to another.

In Papua New Guinea a central aspect of economic and social organisation is the exchange of gifts between clans. One clan will go to great lengths to present its neighbour with, say, a pig, and in return it will receive … a pig! This exchange, which in European eyes may appear bizarre, plays the important role of establishing mutual obligation. Exchange does not discharge a debt, it creates one. The structure of obligations then determines the circulation of daughters between the clans and hence the reproduction of society. The association of human reproduction with exchange is not confined to Melanesia. In Old English the world 'gift' meant 'payment for a wife' and brides are still 'given away'. But while in Papua exchange is central to social survival, the gift economy is not a 'market economy'.

In the Middle Ages the famous fairs of Europe, notably those of the Champagne region of France, provided markets in wine, spices, cloth and money. By the seventeenth century most of the known world was linked by an elaborate mercantile system, centred primarily on Britain and Holland, who were the latest in the long line of trading nations and city states stretching back to antiquity.

But although markets, whether local or international, touched the lives of many, the economies of antiquity, of mediaeval Europe and of the sixteenth and seventeenth centuries were not 'market economies'.

In the Soviet Union today most goods are distributed through the market place of the official stores, with the large GUM store in Moscow playing the role of the great mediaeval fair. But though exchange plays a major role in the economy, no one would call the Soviet Union a 'market economy'.

Production and distribution

What distinguishes a 'market economy' is the way *production* is organised.

The economic life of all societies rests on the solution of two basic problems: the organisation of production and the organisation of distribution.

The organisation of production involves not only the solution of engineering problems – the relations between people and nature – but also the solution of social problems – the relations between people and people: who is to decide how work is organised and what is produced, and who is to do the work.

Organisation of the distribution of the product – who receives what – not only determines who is rich and who is poor, but may also be important in determining who has the power to make economic decisions.

The organisation of production and distribution will be embodied in the fabric of every society – in its institutions, its legal rules and habits and its accepted notions of proper behaviour. Indeed the way the two interdependent problems are solved defines the nature of different systems of economic organisation.

In the textbook example of the feudal manor, the way the economic problem is solved is plain for all to see. The lord of the manor owns the land and provides services for his serfs: a mill, a smithy and protection. The serfs do the work, giving up some of the fruits of their labour to their liege-lord, either directly or in the form of labour services. The whole is bound together by a complex of traditional rights and duties, religious obligation and force. The market, or fair, is the place where excess production may be exchanged for the excess production of others, or for exotic goods and spices. It functions on the edge of economic activity and plays no significant role in the organisation of production.

A quite different solution to the economic problem may be seen today in the Soviet Union. There the land, the factories and the shops are owned by the state, and it is the central planning board which attempts to direct production and distribution. To help solve the distribution problem the state uses markets. Workers are paid money wages, and the state must then fix the prices of goods produced to ensure that workers are able to buy the output designated for their use. Whether this system works well or not is another matter. What is clear is that the role of the market is subsidiary to the decisions of the authorities in the organisation of production.

Therefore in both these dramatically different societies the solution of the economic problem is clearly political. The organisation of production is vested in the political structure of society, and in political power lies the basis of economic decision-making. Economics is about social organisation, about relations between people.

Contrast these societies with the market economy which has characterised economic life in the West for the last two hundred years. In the market economy it is not merely the distribution of some, or even all, of the products which is organised through markets. Production too is organised through the market.

In the market economy all means of production may be bought and sold, and the means are allocated between different lines according to the calculation of profit and loss. In particular, work is organised by the purchase and sale of labour. What truly characterises the market economy is the labour market. Indeed ultimately the market economy is an enormous complex mechanism devoted to the allocation of labour between different tasks.

The market organises production in two distinct ways. First, price calculation signals what lines are likely to be profitable, so the market determines what should be produced. This in turn determines where labour is hired and where workers are laid off. Secondly, while on the factory floor the organisation of production involves complicated social agreements between managers, foremen and workers, in which discipline is applied and accepted or rejected in various ways, the ultimate discipline is the ability to fire workers, to close down plants or to move production elsewhere – to exploit the fact that the workers' livelihood depends on their having jobs, on their being successful in the market place.

If production is to be organised through markets, all means of production must be marketed. The services of land are bought and sold, and so is labour. Therefore, for the market system to emerge from feudalism, land must be liberated from its feudal ties, and labour must be liberated from the land which provided for its needs and instead seek employment for wages. Then not only will the market allocate labour between different trades, but distribution of the product will be organised by the market. For the total product of the country is distributed among its citizens according to the wages, profits and rents which they receive – according, that is, to the services they can sell or the profits they can command.

In the market economy the social and political content of the organisation of production is immersed in the anonymity of the labour market. The ability to organise production and enjoy its fruits is defined by power in the market place. Economic relations between people are therefore determined by their relation to the market.

Your participation in economic life depends on what you have to rent or sell. If all you have to sell is your ability to work, the content of your life is determined by your ability to sell yourself.

So the market solves simultaneously the problems of production and of distribution. What is determined in other economic systems by traditional right and custom and by political power is, in the market system, achieved by buying and selling, no direct contact between the participants being necessary at all. Everyone simply organises his economic life according to the prices of things.

The role of money

The key to the organisation of the production of wealth in the market system is not land, or traditional privilege or political power, but money.

In a system in which everything can be bought and sold, money acquires a peculiar significance that it does not possess in other societies. In the feudal economy land is the basis of economic power; in the Soviet economy economic power is vested in the Party. In both money plays a role in facilitating exchange and the occasional bribe, but it is not *the* determining element in the system.

In the market system, on the other hand, money is economic power. Ownership of money creates the ability not just to purchase output, but to buy inputs, including labour, and set them to work to produce an output that can be sold – for money. We work – for money. Firms produce – for money. Flows of money determine what is produced, where production takes place, who does the work and who receives the fruits of production. The market system is a massive mechanism for the organisation of production, determining the fortunes of countries, regions and towns, and the economic bases of people's lives. And the fuel on which the machine runs is money.

Who controls the operations of this machine? How does it work?

The answer to the first question will be disturbing to some and reassuring to others. Nobody is in control. What is good for General Motors may be good for America, but neither General Motors nor the American government can avoid being buffetted by the storms of the world marketplace. Still less can the British government be said to control Britain's position in the world market or even the operation of the market at home. Economic life in the West is at the mercy of market forces.

And what are these forces? If the market controls and directs our economic fortunes, it would be as well to know how markets work, so that they may be directed, or influenced, to work better.

The desire to understand how the market system worked naturally arose with the market system itself. The market system begat economics.

The origins of economics

Like so many good things, economics originated in France. The first truly scientific economist was François Quesnay (1694-1774), the personal physician of Madame de Pompadour, Louis XV's mistress, at the court of Versailles. Quesnay had written a number of eminent medical treatises, notably one on bleeding, and had nursed the Dauphin through an attack of smallpox, before turning, in his sixties, to the study of economics. His penetrating insights into the workings of the new market system and his careful, yet firm, advocacy of reforms designed to liberate market forces from the constraint of state regulation soon attracted a band of loyal followers. These included the Marquis de Mirabeau and the mercurial Pierre S. Dupont de Nemours who, after the French Revolution, emigrated to America and there founded the great Dupont chemical company. Quesnay's followers constituted the first 'school' of economists, the Physiocrats, so named because they insisted that the propositions they advanced and the policies they advocated were in accord with 'natural law' – thus establishing the tone of omniscient moral rectitude adopted by economists ever since.

Quesnay is best remembered for the analytical methods which he brought ɔ economics, the most famous of which was his *Tableau Economique*, a sort of flow-chart describing the operations of an ideal economy based on an advanced agricultural sector – a situation, he suggested, that was most nearly attained in England. But more important perhaps was how he characterised the operations of the new market system. Quesnay had the knack of capturing the essence of what was going on. Movements of prices were clearly a key element in the working of the new system. In 1756 he observed that the price of a commodity

> varies, and is dependent upon different causes which are as inconstant as they are independent of men's will. This means that the price is not regulated at all by men's needs, and is far from being an arbitrary value or a value which is established by agreement between the contracting parties.

'Independent of men's will ... not regulated at all by men's needs ...', the market had taken over from social and political organisation, from conscious human control. How *did* this revolutionary method of organising production and distribution work?

Adam Smith

The first major attempt to interpret the workings of an *industrial* market system was made by Adam Smith (1723-1790) in his *Inquiry into the Nature and Causes of the Wealth of Nations*, published in 1776. Adam Smith was professor in the Universities of Edinburgh and Glasgow. In the early 1760s he had visited France, where he was greatly influenced by Physiocratic ideas. But he rejected Quesnay's agrarianism and transformed his primitive analytical tools into a sophisticated characterisation of the nascent industrial system *The Wea . of Nations* is one of the great classics of human though ɔr it defin 1 a field of intellectual endeavour. Economics is abou what Adam Smith said it should be about.

At the centre of Adam Smith's scheme was the market. In his attempt to understand the new market system, he began by supposing that *all* production and distribution were organised through markets – a bold and dramatic intellectual leap for 1776 (a year of many bold endeavours, including James Cook's third voyage to the Antipodes, the publication of the first volume of Gibbon's *Decline and Fall of the Roman Empire*, the foundation of the Bolshoi Ballet and the American Declaration of Independence). Certainly it was a less obvious proposition then than it would be today, when markets have permeated so many aspects of daily life, from bought entertainment to bought processed foods.

Adam Smith described how, in such a system, the market would organise production and distribution, flows of money would replace arbitrary power as the directing force of the system, and then, freed of inhibitions, the market would unleash a storm of accumulation. The wealth of the nation would be multiplied, for the new market system was a system of growth and change, of innovation and novelty. The market system would transform the nation and usher in an age of prosperity for all.

If this eminently desirable outcome was to be achieved, three basic reforms were required in the running of the economy.

First, all barriers to the operation of the market must be broken down. In particular all the restrictions on the purchase and sale of labour – the guilds and the apprenticeship regulations of Tudor England – must be abolished. For, argued Adam Smith, they were 'a manifest encroachment upon the just liberty both of the workman and of those who might be disposed to employ him'. Necessary materials must be freely imported. In effect, the government should abolish economic privilege, including its own. Laissez faire should be the new order.

But ability to hire and fire means of production would be of little use if the products could not be sold. If there were no demand for output, producers would be unwilling to risk their capital in production.

So, secondly, markets must be conquered or created. Since conquest is often easier than creation, markets should be opened up at home by improving communications – by building roads and canals. And markets abroad should be opened up by a suitable combination of force and persuasion. Free trade became an economic and a moral necessity – it was 'natural'.

Thirdly, since money was the key to the organisation of

production and distribution, and oiled the wheels of trade, a
financial system was required to finance investment and sales at
home and abroad.

The triumph of the market

In the mid-eighteenth century Britain was already a major trading
nation, with access to foreign markets already attained by conquest,
as in India, or by the careful imposition of superior force, like that
which opened up the markets of her oldest ally, Portugal. The
financial system was well developed, at least in regard to trade, and
the burgeoning empire could provide some of the materials and
purchase part of Britain's production – though what Adam Smith
confidently dismissed as 'the late disturbances' in our North
American colonies heralded difficult times ahead. Moreover, in
Britain, the bonds of feudalism had long been eroded by the growth
of towns and by the agricultural reform – enclosures and the
development of scientific farming – that was an important part of the
new system. Free labourers clogged the roads to the towns in search
of work. Once there, they gathered in the crowded ghettos which,
from the slums of Manchester to the barrios of São Paulo, were to
become the hallmark of a developing labour market. They were the
living essence of the market system. They made it possible.

The foundations were therefore laid for Britain's economic success
in the early nineteenth century, when an industrial revolution was
borne forward by the world-wide demand for basic manufactures
such as iron, and cheap, mass-consumption goods – everyone, after
all, needs clothes. And embedded within the social and economic
institutions of successful, dominant Britain were the ideas and
policies which had liberated the forces of the market and apparently
guaranteed its success: domestic laissez faire, international free trade,
a financial system oriented toward the financing of trade and the
paraphernalia of the Empire.

These were the ingredients of success that formed modern Britain.

The dynamism of the new market system was clearly a challenge
to others. But now, though Britain had given a lead,
industrialisation was less easy. Newcomers had to face the fact that
the powerful British system dominated world markets. So rather
different institutional arrangements had to be devised to counter the
influence of the dynamic and resourceful British. When suitable

arrangements were devised, the labour market and the factory system of organising labour developed rapidly in America, Germany and France; and soon these countries began to challenge British industrial supremacy.

The market system enveloped the world, binding all countries into an interdependent world system. The market system organised labour on a scale never before known, cheapening the cost of mass-produced goods, everywhere stimulating change. The market system changed the world.

Markets penetrated all parts of economic and social life. The products of Birmingham, Essen and Pittsburgh could be found in the most remote parts of the globe. In every home the phrase 'home-made' became less a statement of fact than an advertising slogan attached to factory-produced goods. The accumulative energy released by the market transformed the material and social bounds of everyday life. And everyday life meant the labour market.

The market and Britain's decline

The new solution to the economic problem was forged in Britain. It has been a triumphant success. Some of the costs have been bitter, but in the overall alleviation of human misery the last two hundred years have a unique place in history.

These past achievements, however, brilliant as they may be, are almost blotted out by the images of the present. The fact that everyday life in the modern world is in basic terms 'better' than the life lived by our parents and grandparents, to say nothing of our eighteenth- and nineteenth-century ancestors, is of little immediate relevance to those who face the anxiety and misery of unemployment, or see a life's work ruined by bankruptcy, or wait for two or three years for an operation to correct a painful disability. It is no answer to the overwhelming feeling of waste. Never was anything better named than a 'Depression'.

Throughout its history the market system has been punctuated by cycles of prosperity and depression. But these have usually been set against a background of general advance. The Depression of the 1930s was different, for it heralded a breakdown of the entire system. The economy and polity of liberalism were discredited. Only the war saved the day.

The current state of the West bears disturbing similarities to the inter-war years. All the ingredients are present: falling output, increasing unemployment, an obsession with monetary instability, sabre-rattling ... Even the speeches sound the same. In 1931, as unemployment rose to record heights, Philip Snowden, Chancellor of the Exchequer, argued for cuts in public expenditure and a balanced budget. Further expenditure to alleviate the plight of industry and the unemployed could be financed only by extra taxation, and that was intolerable:

> I say with all the seriousness I can command that the national position is so grave that drastic and disagreeable measures will have to be taken if Budget equilibrium is to be maintained and if industrial progress is to be made. An expenditure which may be easy and tolerable in prosperous times becomes intolerable in a time of grave industrial depression ... I believe ... that an increase of taxation in present conditions which fell on industry would be the last straw. Schemes involving heavy expenditure, however desirable they may be, will have to wait until prosperity returns. This is necessary ... to uphold the present standard of living, and no class will ultimately benefit more by present economy than the wage-earners.

Similar anticipations of current economic thinking may be found in the speeches of Calvin Coolidge and Herbert Hoover, who presided over the debacle in the United States.

It would be premature to predict a world slump on the scale of the 1930s. But from a British perspective it would be a pardonable exaggeration, for the peculiar characteristics of today's British depression not only mirror the conditions of the inter-war years, but – I shall argue – contain portents which are more ominous.

An understanding of Britain's problems requires an understanding of the workings of the market system. Are crises and depressions an inherent characteristic of that system? Or have they been created by the folly of government, or by the pursuit of self-interest allied with the power of corporations or trade unions?

It may seem odd to have begun an investigation of this central contemporary question by reference to eighteenth-century writers and to the market system of the nineteenth century. The West, it might be objected, may still be composed of market economies, but things have changed in the last two hundred years. The economic world is more closely integrated than ever before. Companies are bigger, financial institutions are more sophisticated and, above all, governments play a much greater role in economic affairs. Quite so. But it is not at all evident that these changes have diminished the autonomy of the market. Corporations, banks and trade unions have developed to take greater advantage of the market which is the ultimate arbiter of their success, indeed of their survival. The greater sophistication of its subjects has increased, rather than decreased, the power of the market, circumscribing the role of government. Today, the workings of the market system are, if anything, even more independent of men's will.

The task ahead is now defined. We must confront the market system in terms of the history which has formed it, the institutions which compose it and the ideas which interpret it. To understand what is happening to Britain we need to understand how market economies grow, what determines the level of employment, why there is inflation, why there are balance-of-payments crises, and so on. Are there laws of behaviour guiding this mysterious market mechanism which seems to be in ultimate control of our lives?

To cover all these issues is a tall order for one short book, and the pace will be hot and furious. But there is not much time left. We must understand what is happening and what can be done to resuscitate the British economy, while there is enough of the economy left to resuscitate.

2

Voices in the Air

Economic ideas play an important role in political struggles. Economics grew out of the need to justify handing over control of economic life to the market. Adam Smith's Wealth of Nations *was a manifesto for the market system as an engine of growth. David Ricardo developed the basic analytical method of modern economics in his critique of the Corn Laws. But the classical theory of Smith and Ricardo was based on social class divisions. Once the market system was secure, their ideas were replaced by the more harmonious, neo-classical view, which portrayed the market as an efficient allocator of resources. The new theories also suggested that the labour market automatically adjusts to full employment. Keynes attacked this view. The debate over whether the market is self-adjusting or not is still the fundamental divide in economic theory and policy.*

*   *   *

The ideas of economists and political philosophers, both when they are right and when they are wrong, are more powerful than is commonly understood. Indeed the world is ruled by little else. Practical men, who believe themselves to be quite exempt from any intellectual influences, are usually the slaves of some defunct economist. Madmen in authority, who hear voices in the air, are distilling their frenzy from some academic scribbler of a few years back.

J.M. Keynes, *The General Theory of Employment, Interest and Money* (1936)

Nothing could be more satisfying to the academic than the proposition that his ideas are more important in the global scheme of things than the activities of 'practical men' – the horny-handed, the philistines and the fat cats, who actually do things. Even so, Keynes's estimation of the influence of the academic scribbler contains more than a grain of truth.

For economic organisation and policy is a major field of social and political conflict, and behind every argument in political economy lie not only vested interests but real disagreements about how the market economy actually works. Economics has developed out of these intellectual and political struggles over the past two hundred years. From the debates over the Corn Laws and nineteenth-century free trade to Roosevelt's New Deal and modern monetarism, a fundamental source of disagreement – whatever the particular issue – has been: How do markets work?

Such ideas as we have of the workings of the market system have been fabricated and assembled by economists. The role of prices, the concept of efficiency, the place of the individual in society, the significance of monetary calculation – all these have been the object of some economic theory or other. The words and ideas of economists form our understanding of the economy. So, before we can proceed with the business in hand – the life and hard times of the British economy – we must take a Grand Tour through the ideas, defunct and not-so-defunct, that haunt us today. These ideas have been developed over the last two hundred years in an attempt to reveal the workings of the market system.

The market and economics

The market economy is a mysterious thing. It is a system in which, in principle, all economic life – all production, all distribution – is organised through buying and selling; in which flows of money determine the scale, location and content of economic life; in which vitally inter-related decisions are made by countless individuals and companies on the basis of price calculations alone, with little or no direct communication among themselves.

Now, in a local area, with a limited number of people involved, this might be a plausible picture. But from its very beginnings the market system has operated on a world scale. The industrial revolution was built on cotton, a raw material brought from the New

World, processed in Britain and then sold all over the globe.

At least as important, therefore, as the eighteenth- and nineteenth-century technological innovations we all learn about at school – the spinning jenny, Crompton's mule, Watt's steam engine and so on – were the changes in economic organisation that gathered pace in the eighteenth century and then swept aside the old system of economic organisation.

The making of knives, forks and spoons had been controlled in Sheffield by the Cutlers' Company. The company was incorporated by Act of Parliament in 1624, so that regulations which had been built up over the preceding hundred years were given the force of law. Membership of the company required an apprenticeship of seven years under a Master, and as each Master was allowed only one apprentice at a time, the quantity – as well as the quality – of output was strictly controlled.

Moreover Company regulations in 1662 prohibited members from buying the components for making knives from anyone who was not also a member of the Company. The Company even had its own police force, the Searchers, who by a statute of 1625 were authorised 'from time to time to enter into any house or houses, shops, cellars or warehouses, of the said Company, to search for deceitful wares and for those who work, buy or sell contrary to the statute'.

But by the end of the eighteenth century the power of the guilds and corporations was on the wane. By 1806 the effective power of the Cutlers' Company had gone, and with it the mechanism of controls on production and trade which characterised Tudor England.

The system of controls had been complex, though it is easy to see how it worked. Now it was swept away and replaced by – nothing. Length of apprenticeship could no longer be used to limit production, and quality was no longer regulated by statute: instead, the final arbiter was to be the market.

What effect would this abdication to the market have? Anarchy and chaos, it might reasonably have been supposed.

Yet this was not so. The market system may be successful or unsuccessful. It may unleash a boom of innovative activity, or it may perpetuate an enduring slump. But it isn't chaos. It *is* a system with its own internal laws of behaviour – laws which regulate, co-ordinate, direct and discipline all participants in the market economy: that is, everyone. The laws are there, demanding to be revealed.

At least that is what all economists believe!

If the market system is guided by hidden laws, we ought to know what they are. Perhaps they can be manipulated to achieve desirable results: full employment, for example, or a respectable rate of growth. Some sort of analytical apparatus is required to dig beneath the surface complexities and reveal just what these laws are. Economics is supposed to provide this apparatus.

Economics and politics

But economic ideas do not arise from simple intellectual curiosity. When vested interests in society clash, ideas are one of the weapons used in the struggle. A group putting forward a particular point of view will try to show not only that it has a uniquely correct understanding of how the system works, but also that, as a consequence, its policies conform to 'natural justice', or are in the 'national interest'. Economic analysis thus plays a vital role in political controversy. But it would be wrong to imagine that this role is pursued entirely cynically. Economists' ideas do not lead events, they follow them. Brilliant political fashions are often economically old-hat. Ideas are picked up, dropped, revived, given more attractive covering (mathematics being the fashionable top-dressing at the moment) and presented as penetrating and new. Nothing is quite so powerful as an idea whose time has come.

Therefore, once a particular interpretation has been invented of how the system works, it may be transformed and developed in a way which is totally independent of the conflict in which it originated. An idea which began merely as an argument in a particular cause acquires a 'scientific aspect'. It appears to be independent of political controversy, and so becomes a yet more powerful propaganda weapon.

Although economists are often the intellectual hired guns of political interests, this does not mean that they don't sometimes identify some elements of the process by which the market mechanism actually works. But it does mean that we should always be aware of just where ideas come from. For even the most abstract bit of theorising is erected round the skeleton of its ideological origins.

Adam Smith and the birth of the market economy

The birth of the market economy was painful and slow. The infant was almost stifled at birth by the vested interests that were themselves threatened by the rise of the market – the remnants of feudal privilege, the guilds, the companies trading under Royal patent and the 'landed interest'. Adam Smith's *Wealth of Nations* provided the intellectual ammunition in the battle for market freedom.

The Cutlers' Company was cited by Adam Smith as a typical example of the 'corporations' which regulated production and trade, restrained competition and were, all in all, 'a conspiracy against the public'. He was particularly incensed by the apprenticeship regulations, based on the Elizabethan Statute of Apprenticeship, which enacted that no person 'should for the future exercise any trade, craft, or mystery at that time exercised in England, unless he had previously served to it an apprenticeship of seven years at least'. All monopolies, rights and privileges, including the rights of workers, were to be swept aside and every individual and company left to fend for itself in the market place. The new freedom would release a wave of innovative endeavour, raising the rate of growth. Roads and canals would be built – opening up new markets, raising demand for the products of the new factories, encouraging technical change through the division of labour, enhancing the wealth and power of the nation.

The market, moreover, would not be anarchic, but would provide a mechanism of co-ordination, directing individual self-interest toward social benefit through the driving force of competition. The struggle for more, enforced by competition, would ensure that resources flowed to areas in which they might most profitably be used, and that new techniques were adopted that cheapened production. Anyone who refused to take the plunge would be swept aside. Competition produced change, novelty, innovation and growth; competition produced wealth. Adam Smith's book was a manifesto for the new market system.

In the early years of the nineteenth century the conflict over the liberation of free market forces focussed on one clear-cut issue: free trade – or, more precisely, free trade in corn. The campaign for the abolition of the Corn Laws was a political struggle between, on the one hand, agriculture, the landlords and the countryside – the past –

and, on the other, industry, manufacturers and their workers, and the towns – the future. The agricultural interests campaigned for restrictions to be maintained on the importation of corn, so that the price of domestic grain would be kept high. The industrial interests wanted imports of cheap foreign grain, so that the pressure on wages would be reduced and the profits that would fund new investment, and hence future growth, raised. As in any major economic struggle, each side had economists arguing its case.

Ricardo and the manufacturing classes

The chief economist supporting the industrial classes was David Ricardo (1772-1823), a brilliant young stockbroker who, having made his fortune on the Exchange, bought several large country estates and in his early forties turned to politics (he became an M.P. in 1819) and to the study of economic theory. In 1815 he published a pamphlet entitled *An Essay on the Influence of a low Price of Corn on the Profits of Stock shewing the Inexpediency of Restrictions on Importation*, which proved to be a best-seller, a second printing being required only a few days after the first. This was not, as hindsight might suggest, because it was destined to become a classic in economic analysis, but rather because it was a fundamental attack on the Corn Laws and on the economic arguments of the landlords. 'The interest of the landlord,' Ricardo was to write later, 'is always opposed to that of the consumer and the manufacturer.'

Ricardo's argument was built on two basic propositions: first, that the wage of each worker was given at, or near, subsistence; secondly, that the surplus produced over and above the wage was distributed between landlords and capitalists in the form of rents and profits according as land was scarce or plentiful.

The Corn Laws, by prohibiting the import of foreign grain, kept up the demand for expensive home-produced gain and so raised the rent that landlords could command for the use of their land. High rents bit into profits, cutting investment and growth. As the economy grew, the number of industrial workers would grow with it. Since the workers' subsistence was based on grain, the pressure on domestic agricultural resources would rise, forcing rents yet higher and cutting profits yet further. Ultimately, increasing rents would bring growth to a painful halt.

If the Corn Laws were abolished, on the other hand, the price of corn and the level of rents would both fall, and profits would rise. The growing industrial labour force could be fed from the wheatlands of the world, and there would be no limit on the growth of the economy. Everyone would benefit – even perhaps, in the end, the landlords – from the greater prosperity.

Implicit in Ricardo's case was the assumption that the social classes played different roles in the economy. The workers merely subsisted; the landlords squandered their share of the product in riotous living, indulgence in the delights of the countryside, and in wine, persons and song; the capitalists accumulated. Therefore the greater the share that went to the capitalists, the greater the level of investment, and hence the greater the rate of growth.

This characterisation of the role of social classes was not peculiar to Ricardo, but was broadly accepted by all economists at the time, including those who attempted to defend the Corn Laws and the role of the landlords. (The champion of the landlords' interest was T.R. Malthus (1766-1834), famous for his pessimistic *Essay on the Principle of Population*, of whom more later. Smith, Ricardo, Malthus and John Stuart Mill (1806-1873) were the leading figures of what has come to be known as the English School of Classical Political Economy, one of the interesting characteristics of which is that none of these leading figures was English. Smith, Malthus and Mill were all Scots, and Ricardo was of Dutch-Portuguese ancestry, his father having emigrated from Amsterdam in about 1760.)

Ricardo's argument was presented in a system of precise mathematical logic, in terms of what is now called a 'model'. Construction of a model involves abstracting from reality what are believed to be the most relevant factors that affect a particular situation, and working out their relationships and interactions within the analytical vacuum. The clarity of Ricardo's argument rested on key simplifying assumptions – that the wages of the workers, for example, might be regarded as consisting only of corn – without which the antagonism between rents and profits would have been difficult to reveal unambiguously. In economics there is always a temptation to choose assumptions that are convenient rather than realistic – a vice that afflicts all economists, though some more than others. But, as was shown after his time, Ricardo's results do not depend on his rather limiting assumptions. In particular, the idea for which he was to be most criticised – that profits are determined by the surplus of output over wages – has been triumphantly vindicated. Analytical model-building has been the method of economic theorising ever since Ricardo wrote. Adam Smith had defined what economics was about. Ricardo showed how it was to be done.

The debate over the Corn Laws was not resolved for another thirty years, and remained a bitter, divisive element in British politics. But when abolition eventually came, it proved to be something of an anti-climax. Agriculture was not ruined. On the contrary, the growing urban economy ensured an expanding demand for home-produced agricultural goods for the next twenty years, until British arable farming was overwhelmed by competition from the prairies. Moreover many of the landlords had themselves invested in mines, or canals, or manufacturing, and the lines of the old class conflict between Land and Capital became blurred.

Capital and labour

Ricardo's ideas expressed the economic philosophy of the manufacturing classes. But as the nineteenth century wore on and the conflict between Land and Capital faded into history, a new and more bitter conflict began to dominate social and political life, the conflict between Capital and Labour. This created a problem for the economists. For, despite his eminent respectability, Ricardo had, as an incidental part of his analysis, portrayed wages and profits, as well as profits and rents, as mutually antagonistic. From the point of view of those in authority the growth of the trade-union movement, and the emerging political demands of an increasingly self-confident working class gathering into socialist parties, did not sit well with an economics that suggested that the operations of the market economy should be seen in terms of class conflict. As early as 1831 economists could be found who were prepared to accuse Ricardo and his followers 'not merely or errors, but of crimes', for:

> In their theory of rent, they have insisted that landlords can thrive only at the expense of the public at large, and especially of the capitalists: in their theory of profits, they have declared that capitalists can only improve their circumstances by depressing those of the labouring and numerous class: ... In one and all of their arguments they have studiously exhibited the interests of every class in society as necessarily at perpetual

variance with every other class! (G.P. Scrope, *Quarterly Review*, November 1831)

It was Karl Marx who took up the theoretical tools forged by Ricardo in the interests of the capitalists and transformed them in such a way as to expose the true class conflict and repression on which the market system was based, charting that system's internal contradictions and revealing the substance of its ultimate self-created destruction. The bourgeois economics of Smith and Ricardo culminated in a set of ideas that haunted the privileged and the powerful, ideas that inspired revolutionary movements committed to the *rejection* of the market system. From the Paris Commune of 1871 to the Russian Revolution in 1917 and Mao's China, classical economics has contributed to the philosophy that has threatened the market.

Neo-classical theory

This would not do. A new, more soothing economics was required. The search was on for new economic ideas which would not portray the market as an arena of conflict but show instead that the market system operates harmoniously, in everyone's best interest. As luck would have it, such ideas had in fact already been developed, though their significance has been obscured by the weight of Ricardian orthodoxy. They were now eagerly taken up and became the basis for an entirely new theory of the workings of the market system.

The new ideas had been developed in their essentials in the 1850s by a German writer, Heinrich Gossen (1810-1858), who claimed that his innovations in economics were on a par with those of Copernicus in astronomy. But their time had not yet come, and Gossen remains a shadowy, unfulfilled figure in the history of economics.

The *annus mirabilis* was 1871, when the new theory burst onto the academic scene throughout continental Europe. Independently of one another Carl Menger (1840-1921) in Vienna, Léon Walras (1834-1910) in Lausanne and Stanley Jevons (1835-1882) in Manchester presented what were fundamentally the same new principles of economics. The new system would, Jevons believed, 'overthrow many of the principal doctrines of the Ricardo-Mill Economics' and replace the 'mazy and preposterous assumptions of the Ricardian School'. The market was now to be construed as an engine, not of conflict, but of harmony and fairness:

> Every labourer [wrote Jevons] ultimately receives the due value of his produce after paying a proper fraction to the capitalist for the remuneration of abstinence and risk.

Codified by Alfred Marshall (1842-1924), refined and expanded, the new theory remains the economic orthodoxy to this day, dominating the teaching of economics in Western universities to a degree rivalled only by the teaching of orthodox Marxism in the economics departments of Eastern Europe. It is the very cornerstone of modern monetarism, and of much of the thinking that underlies the policies of most Western governments.

Though it attracted the label 'neo-classical', the new theoretical system was completely different from the old. The basic units of economic life were no longer social classes, but individuals. The market brings them together in what is seen as a massive auction, in which they swap the goods and services with which nature has endowed them (including the ability to work) in an attempt to acquire a more desirable package. Ability to work might be traded for food, for example. As in an auction, this multi-lateral swap-shop is supposed to result in the formation of rates of exchange – prices – which balance the amount of a particular good that some wish to offer with the amount that others demand. Thus the market ensures that the quantity offered is always the quantity bought.

This picture applies not only to auctions of cattle and antiques, but also to labour and capital. Just as the farmer brings cows and pigs to auction, so the worker brings his labour and the capitalist his capital, each seeking the best price he can get and receiving what others are willing to pay. The wage therefore represents the market's estimation of what the worker is worth – 'the due value of his produce' – and capital receives what *it* is worth – its 'proper fraction'. What labour and capital are worth will be determined by the aggregated demands of individual consumers. What consumers will be willing to pay will be determined by the relationship between the intensity of their desire to acquire the products of labour and capital, and the amounts of labour and capital that are available to satisfy those desires.

The market has to co-ordinate all these attempts to buy and sell. Although in a modern economy this is an extremely complex operation, the new theorists claimed that it was no different in principle from the cattle market. So all commodities that are produced will find a buyer – at a price. And, which is more important, everyone who wishes to work will find a job – at some wage or other. The market is a massive self-adjusting mechanism that ensures full employment.

Moreover the market is *efficient*.

The mechanism of efficiency

Adam Smith and the classical economists had argued that the market was more efficient than the old system of controls, for competition would force the pace of technical change and the lowering of production costs. But when the new economists argued that the market was efficient, they meant something quite different.

The neo-classical economists' idea of efficiency derived from their image of the market system as a conglomeration of individuals all trying to improve their particular situations by trade – to maximise, as they put it, their utility. If everyone was given the liberty to buy and sell wherever fancy led, everyone would arrange sales and purchases in such a way as to maximise utility – and surely that was a Good Thing. So the market led to efficiency by being the mechanism through which everyone might maximise the utility to be derived from the abilities and wealth with which they had been endowed by nature.

But this result contains an awkward conclusion. If the market leads to efficiency for each individual, can it not also lead to social efficiency – to the maximisation of utility in society as a whole? Since the amount of utility to be derived from any extra income clearly depends on the amount of income you have in the first place, the overall sum of social utility will be enhanced by taking from the rich, who won't suffer too much of a loss, and giving to the poor, who will benefit from their gain. Therefore the highest level of social utility will be attained if income is evenly spread throughout the economy. The new economists, who were portraying the market system as socially harmonious, seemed also to be proposing a remarkably egalitarian social programme.

A way out of this difficulty was suggested by the Oxford professor Francis Ysidro Edgeworth (1845-1926). The rich have a greater capacity for pleasure than the poor and so derive greater utility from any extra income they may acquire:

Capacity for pleasure is a property of evolution [wrote Edgeworth] an essential attribute of civilization. The grace of life, the charm of courtesy and courage, which once at least distinguished rank, rank not unreasonably received the means to enjoy and to transmit. To the lower classes the works of which they seemed most capable; the work of the higher classes being different in kind was not to be equated in severity ... The aristocracy of sex is similarly grounded upon the supposed superior capacity of the man for happiness.

A somewhat more convincing argument was advanced by Vilfredo Pareto (1848-1923), who pointed out that not only was the idea of adding up utilities rather silly (how are they to be measured – in utils? And how do *my* utils compare with *your* utils?), but the new theories worked perfectly well without trying to add them up. The only assumption the theory needed was that each individual maximised whatever he wanted to maximise. This, at least, was something to say in favour of the market. Nothing could or should be said about the distribution of income.

But the idea that the market is efficient in some general social sense exercises a powerful appeal none the less. The market is an efficient mechanism for allocating scarce resources between alternative uses; for ensuring that scarce labour will be directed toward its most useful tasks; for ensuring full employment.

Employment and unemployment

The issue of employment and unemployment had not figured prominently in the work of Smith and Ricardo, who had viewed it as but an aspect of economic growth. Could the economy grow fast enough to absorb a working class that seemed so intent on reproducing itself?

Whether it could or not, it was assumed that the drive to accumulate would always ensure that all machines were fully employed, even if the people were not. Malthus, Ricardo's main opponent, attempted to refute this optimistic conclusion by suggesting that ability to produce would run ahead of demand and thus that a wealthy landlord class was necessary to keep up demand by performing the social duty of extravagant consumption. But

Malthus could not put together a coherent argument. Ricardo and the industrialists carried the day.

The new economics, however, does offer a theory of full employment of labour and of machines. Since the market balances all demands and all offers, the labour brought to market must be sold. There may be short-term mistakes and miscalculations, but as long as the workings of the market are not inhibited – by trade unions, for example, or monopolistic price setters – the self-adjusting mechanism will maintain full employment.

This was the still core of the economic thinking of academics and politicians, bankers and businessmen in 1932. In that year there were $2\frac{3}{4}$ million unemployed in Britain, 13.5 per cent of the labour force. Labour was not scarce, and was clearly not being efficiently allocated. Something had gone terribly wrong.

The Great Depression of the 1930s was a crisis for society, and a crisis for economics too. The economists argued desperately that unemployment was a temporary phenomenon which the self-adjusting market should eventually eliminate. The explanation of prolonged unemployment must therefore be that the market was being prevented from doing its job. Wages were too high; so the demand for labour was cut off, leaving many unemployed. And high levels of government expenditure were absorbing too much of the nation's limited savings, which could be far better allocated by the private sector according to the dictates of the market. The government, accepting this analysis as correct, forced wage-cuts and reduced its own spending – and the depression deepened. The market must be allowed to work!

Keynes

John Maynard Keynes (1883-1946) did not agree. At the time, Keynes was probably the only living economist of whom the ordinary educated person had ever heard. His *Economic Consequences of the Peace* (1919) had dissected the rapacious Treaty of Versailles, which had concluded the First World War by imposing totally unrealistic reparations on Germany, and exposed the foibles of Lloyd George, Orlando, Woodrow Wilson and Clemenceau, who between them had fashioned the 'nightmare'.

Throughout the inter-war period Keynes struggled to make sense of the cumulative decline of the British economy and the folly of government policies. What was needed, he argued, was a programme of public works to stimulate employment. In calling for expansionary policies Keynes was not alone. Some more orthodox economists – deserting, in desperation, their own economic principles – joined in too. The authorities were content to rest on the orthodox view and to point out the analytical inconsistencies of arguments for increased government expenditure. In a 1929 White Paper the Treasury argued that expenditure on public works would divert labour from 'normal industry', absorb savings that were better used by private enterprise and cause inflation. What was needed was cuts in wages and government expenditure, increased industrial efficiency and rationalisation.

Keynes exposed the theoretical underpinning of the Treasury View in a radio talk entitled 'Poverty in Plenty: Is the Economic System Self-Adjusting', broadcast in 1934. He portrayed economists as falling into two groups:

> On the one side [he said] are those who believe that the existing economic system is, in the long run, a self-adjusting system, though with creaks and groans and jerks, and interrupted by time lags, outside interference and mistakes ... on the other side of the gulf are those who reject the idea that the existing economic system is, in any significant sense, self-adjusting ...
>
> The strength of the self-adjusting school depends on its having behind it almost the whole body of organised economic thinking and doctrine of the last hundred years. This is a formidable power. It is the product of acute minds and has persuaded and convinced the great majority of the intelligent and disinterested persons who have studied it. It has vast prestige and a more far-reaching influence than is obvious. For it lies behind the education and the habitual modes of thought, not only of economists, but of bankers and businessmen and civil servants and politicians of all parties ...
>
> Thus, if the heretics on the other side of the gulf are to demolish the forces of nineteenth-century orthodoxy ... they must attack them in their citadel. No successful attack has yet been made ...
>
> I range myself with the heretics.

Not only is Britain today repeating the economic history of the

Depression, but the economic controversy of the Depression is being repeated too. Once again on one side are those who believe that the market system is self-adjusting and on the other those who, for a variety of reasons, believe that it is not. The former include – indeed are dominated by – the monetarists. The latter are a more heterogeneous group, but a majority would probably refer to themselves as 'Keynesians'.

The attack on the citadel of orthodox theory was made by Keynes in his *General Theory of Employment, Interest and Money*, published in 1936. Keynes argued that the orthodox view of how the market system works was completely wrong. There was no mechanism which guaranteed that the level of demand for commodities would be sufficient to ensure that labour would be fully employed producing them. First, the labour market did not work in the way the orthodox economists suggested. Cutting wages when there are people unemployed would only make matters worse by reducing the purchasing power of those who still had a job. Secondly, the idea that government expenditure preempted part of a given amount of saving was equally fallacious. Saving depended on income. If government expenditure was increased, incomes would rise and savings would rise too. Government spending did not preempt anything. It set idle resources to work when the market would not. Thirdly, increased spending on investment by businessmen was limited not by saving but by the availability of finance (would the bank provide the loan to invest in a new factory and new machines?) and by the prospect of profit. If businessmen invested the levels of employment, incomes and savings would rise.

The level of employment depended on the level of demand – of demand for consumer goods and for investment goods: machines, factories and the like. Consumer demand, which varied with income, was not, on its own, sufficient to maintain a full-employment level of demand. The key factor in fluctuations in demand, therefore, was fluctuations in investment. But even if the finance was available, there was no reason why businessmen should take the risk of investing if they were not confident of future profit. Workers and machines would simply lie idle. Even cheap labour and cheap resources were not worth using if the product could not be sold. The market mechanism did not, and could not, ensure that the economy operated at full employment.

If the market could not ensure that there was sufficient demand from consumers and investors to give full employment, the state must step in to make up the difference – or, at least, by means of tax cuts and subsidies, stimulate private spending. So Keynes's analysis provided the theoretical justification for the intervention of the state in the operation of the economy – intervention that would take place 'in the national interest'. Many 'heretics' had advocated intervention before, but now the argument was given intellectual weight – and intellectual coherence.

In recent years the theoretical force of Keynes's arguments has been reinforced by a critique of the logic of the arguments of the self-adjusting school, put forward by an Italian economist, Piero Sraffa (1898-), who has lived most of his life in England after being expelled from Italy by Mussolini in 1927. In a book entitled enigmatically *Production of Commodities by Means of Commodities*, published in 1960, Sraffa pointed out that while the idea of supply and demand for labour or land might appear to make sense, that same idea, when applied to capital, ran into severe analytical difficulties. For what is capital? A collection of machines? But the stock of machines is continually changing. An amount of money? But it makes no sense to regard money as a means of production. There is no way of specifying what capital is that fits in with the supply-and-demand analysis of the determination of the rate of profit. And if the rate of profit is not determined by supply and demand, then the prices of all commodities into which profits enter are not determined by supply and demand either! The subsequent controversy has been conducted at a high level of abstraction over the past two decades. It culminated in an admission by the high priest of orthodoxy, Paul Samuelson, that Sraffa was right – something is logically wrong with neo-classical theory.

The abstract level of Sraffa's argument has tended to obscure the dramatic significance of his point. It amounts to saying that the self-adjusting school is without theoretical foundation. But in recent years the ideas of the neo-classical self-adjusting school have come back into fashion. They have even succeeded, as we shall see, in emasculating and then absorbing Keynes's ideas. But Sraffa's conclusion has proved less digestible, and so has not been popular in many quarters. Like most unpopular propositions, it has been assiduously ignored.

Is the market self-adjusting?

The way Keynes's ideas were used in formulating government policy during and after the Second World War, and the motives lying behind the more recent rejection of those ideas by so many governments, are topics to be dealt with later. For the moment it cannot be emphasised too strongly that the issue we have identified – is the market self-adjusting or is it not? – is the fundamental issue in the debate over British economic policy today. Whether it be inflation, employment, international trade, the organisation and management of nationalised industries, the role of the welfare state, the role of education and the health service, or any major economic issue you can think of, the underlying arguments can generally be clearly identified by means of this 'self-adjustment' litmus paper.

One complication in this simple method of sorting out the sheep from the goats is the presence of a large group of mongrels, who argue that the market would be self-adjusting if only it were not prevented from being so by institutional characteristics of the real world – the power of trade unions and corporations, for example – or by the pervasive effects of uncertainty about the future. Although such arguments are pragmatically appealing and allow their proponents to masquerade as sensible fellows who look at the facts, they are fundamentally incoherent when it comes to the formation of policy and, in intellectual controversy, easy meat for the self-adjusters. If powerful institutions inhibit the workings of the market, should the state intervene in the market, or should it attack the power of vested interests (pass laws to weaken trade unions, for example, or break up big companies) and allow society to reap the benefit of an efficient market? As for uncertainty, every person and every company has to develop some method for dealing with the uncertain future we all face. If the market is a systematically self-adjusting mechanism, that method must reflect the real characteristics of the market. If it did not, the method would be shown to be consistently wrong, and no one but the most perverse dogmatist, would adopt behaviour that was consistently wrong. So, although uncertainty may from time to time toss a self-adjusting market off course, it does not introduce any fundamental change into the workings of the market mechanism – so long, that is, as we believe that the mechanism is there in the first place.

The debate therefore is really only two-sided. Do markets work to achieve an efficient allocation of resources via the operation of the price mechanism? Or, even in the best of all possible worlds (that is, giving the self-adjusters all the assumptions they may wish about absence of trade unions, big companies and so on), does the market not work that way? This is a crucial debate, for although it is often conducted in abstract terms and with all the analytical complexities which enhance the most banal propositions, it is a debate which affects politics and policies – which affects people's lives. No issue is so sensitive, and rightly, as the issue of unemployment. For unemployment is waste – waste of resources and waste of lives. If the market ensures full employment, let it thrive. If it does not, something must be done.

But what? Can jobs be conjured out of thin air? In the long run, whether there are jobs or not depends on the growth of the economy, on the building of new factories producing new products which *sell*. In the current debate over unemployment the old classical concern with growth has been somewhat lost. But there is an intimate relationship between growth and employment, a relationship that for Britain has proved nearly fatal.

3

The Principle of Cumulative Causation

Success in the market system means keeping up with the pace of change, maintaining competitiveness. The growth of manufacturing is the key·element. Competitiveness in manufactured goods depends more on non-price factors, such as quality and design, than on price alone, and both are favourably influenced by a high rate of growth of productivity. The rate of growth of productivity is determined by the rate of growth of demand for manufactures. So demand determines competitiveness determines demand. This is cumulative causation. The dynamic of cumulative causation may be broken by institutional rigidity or set in motion by institutional innovation. The interaction between cumulative causation and institutional change is the basis of the nineteenth-century origins of Britain's decline.

* * *

Of all British inventions, none has done so much to change the world as the industrial market system.

Once the organisation of economic life was seized by the market, nothing would ever be the same again. The powerful dynamic set in motion by the combined forces of individual self-interest, competition and the development of new methods of production broke through institutional barriers. It tore people from their traditional ways of life, transforming town and countryside and steadily absorbing the entire world. (Some parts of the world, notably the Soviet Union, later broke away from the market system and attempted to set up an entirely different system for organising production and distribution. Whether this has been a success or failure is a contentious story that cannot be told here.)

Industry requires raw materials and labour. Reserves of copper, zinc, coal and oil, wherever they might be, had therefore to be gathered into the ambit of the market, and the peasantry in the countryside and the artisans in the towns had to be converted into an industrial labour force.

Industry needs to sell, and so industrial goods had to penetrate every aspect of human existence. The urban markets of the artisans had to be absorbed. Native artefacts had to be produced in Birmingham or, more probably, Hong Kong. Rural cottage industry disappeared, unable to compete with the factory, as did home production of everything from bread to entertainment. And this penetration everywhere released more and more labour for the factories.

In the market system, in which money is the fount of economic power, flows of money round the world organise and direct the productive energies of labour and machines. Monetary calculation defines economic life. *Aurum vincit omnia.*

The pace of change

As the influence of the market system spread, so the pace of change quickened. The competitive struggle forced producers on to greater and greater efforts to outstrip rivals in innovation and novelty. The scientific content of the industrial revolution was relatively old-hat. Steam engines and the new textile machinery were not based on new ideas in science, but on the practical application of well-known principles. Today the gap between scientific research and industrial innovation has shrunk dramatically. Even the most abstract findings in low-temperature physics or biochemistry are rapidly translated into new competitive products. Scientific research, for many companies, has become a competitive strategy. Science has been taken from its ivory tower and thrust into the market place.

Not only does the bundle of commodities produced change more and more rapidly. So does the place in which they are produced, the way they are produced and the people who produce them. As the pace of change quickens, machines become outdated. Towns and whole regions enjoy bursts of prosperity followed by decay. Hard-won skills become irrelevant. People become obsolete.

The organisation of production changes too. Small owner-managed firms are replaced by large corporations which can more easily mobilise and direct large flows of money, the primary agent of change.

Today, even in a slump, the pace of change is probably quicker than ever before. We only have to look around us. The industrial market system creates change, real or imagined, for good or ill.

Booms and slumps

The process by which the market system has come to dominate the economic life of most of the world has not been smooth. The expansion of the system has proceeded in fits and starts, punctuating the development of individual countries with sometimes catastrophic recessions, which have ruined businesses and ruined lives. The most serious was the Great Depression of the 1930s, which only Germany and the Soviet Union, and to some extent Japan, escaped by cutting themselves off from the markets of the rest of the world. Today the world system is displaying some of the same characteristics, and the ideas being touted by many economists, and the policies of most governments, are chillingly reminiscent of the ideas and policies which were popular then.

Uneven development

But Britain's problems are not derived primarily from the world recession. The weakness of the British economy, which has been so cruelly exposed by the problems that have afflicted the Western economies in the past decade, is the cumulative product of the entire history of Britain since the war – indeed, of the entire history of Britain since the end of the nineteenth century, when it first became evident that Britain was unable, or unwilling, to adapt to a competitive world in which her pre-eminence could no longer be taken for granted. Of fundamental relevance, therefore, to Britain's current plight is that not only does the world system develop in fits and starts, but it does not grow evenly between regions or countries. Rather than other countries catching up with Britain and the entire system then advancing on its way in a uniform and orderly manner, one country after another has achieved prominence in the more dynamic industrial activities of the day – with the former leaders slipping back into subordination, or even into stagnation and decay.

Britain started the whole process off, but by the mid-nineteenth century income per head had risen higher in the United States and, a decade or so later, in Germany. By the end of the century Britain had been overtaken by Australia, Canada and Argentina, though the latter's brilliance was short-lived.

The United States established a huge lead in income per head as a result of a consistently high rate of growth in the nineteenth century and the early years of the twentieth century. Since the war, however, this lead has been steadily eroded, especially in manufacturing industry. Output of manufactures per head is now higher in Germany, Sweden, France and Belgium.

It is here, in the stuttering rhythm of rise and fall which has punctuated the last two hundred years, that we can perhaps find a clue to the underlying character of Britain's current economic problems.

The role of manufacturing

In the nineteenth century the key to prosperity was clearly the growth of manufacturing industry. Manufacturing was the symbol of the new era. It captured the imagination, and provided the theme for the economists and philosophers of the new order. Iron artefacts became fashionable, elegant iron candlesticks replacing silver and brass. The engineer Isambard Kingdom Brunel was a national hero. Manufacturing was progress: progress was manufacturing.

The same is true today. Successful manufacturing industry is everywhere the basis of national prosperity and economic dynamism. Other sectors of the economy, such as agriculture, mining, construction and services like retailing, banking and insurance, all make a substantial contribution to the *level* of well-being. But manufacturing is the key to *growth*.

Even countries which developed initially as food and raw material suppliers to the industrial world, such as New Zealand, Australia, Canada and South Africa, have attained a sustained growth of real incomes only through the development of their manufacturing industry. Likewise the failure of Argentina is due to her failure to develop a viable manufacturing base. Countries wealthy by chance, such as the members of OPEC, or by convenience, such as tax-havens of off-shore banking in the Cayman Islands, prove the rule. For it would never be suggested that these activities have in them the stuff of sustained economic growth. Their prosperity ultimately depends on the health of the industrial economies.

Why manufacturing?

Manufacturing industry possesses a unique combination of three characteristics which are the very essence of sustained economic progress.

First, there is an almost infinite demand for manufactured goods. Not only do manufactures replace handicrafts and production in the home, but as income rises the demand for manufactures rises yet more rapidly, both because people want more manufactures as such and because so many of the other goods and services that we buy acquire a larger and larger manufactured component. Agricultural products are now highly 'manufactured' before they reach the dining table. So are services. Think, for example, of the number of manufactures involved in the production of a successful package holiday.

Secondly, there is an unlimited scope for technical change in manufacturing industry. Today's processes and commodities are yesterday's science fiction. Micro-electronics, robots, video-recorders, new synthetics – the list is endless and ever-changing. It would be difficult today to find any manufactured product that existed in 1950; and if such can be found (standard food products are the most likely survivors) they will not have been made in the same way as then. More and more comes from less and less. In particular, the amount of labour required to produce any particular manufacture steadily diminishes.

Thirdly, and most significant of all, manufacturing embodies a peculiar internal dynamic, whereby change promotes demand, which in turn promotes change. Innovation in production and the ability to sell, which is the *sine qua non* of successful production, feed on and stimulate one another. This relationship is easy to see whenever there is a dramatic new innovation in manufacturing, such as the introduction of electric power. The new power source poses new demands throughout industry: machinery must be replaced, new methods and techniques must be adopted. Moreover the introduction of electricity leads, in turn, to the introduction of a wide variety of entirely new products, many of which satisfy new needs. These changes on the production and the demand side in turn stimulate further product changes, reorganisations of production and so on. What may be seen in particularly dramatic form in the case of electricity applies in essence to the countless small changes in products and methods that characterise the day-to-day working of manufacturing industry. Quite minor changes can ramify throughout the various sectors of industry, unexpectedly stimulating activity at several removes from the initial impulse.

The mutual reinforcement of production and demand is the distinctive attribute of manufacturing. Manufacturing shares a high growth rate of demand with services. Demand for agricultural products tends to tail off as income rises. But in agriculture, as in industry, there is enormous scope for technical progress. Indeed British agriculture since the war has consistently enjoyed a higher rate of productivity growth than manufacturing – albeit by the use of more and more manufactures down on the farm. Services have less scope for technical improvement, apart from what comes via manufacturing, such as the introduction of computers. There are occasional major improvements in the services sector – the development of supermarkets in retailing, for example – but these are relatively rare events, and certainly cannot provide a basis for sustained economic growth.

Sustained growth derives from the combination of all three factors, and particularly from the self-reinforcing dynamic which is the peculiar characteristic of manufacturing.

Moreover, not only is manufacturing capable of sustained growth in and of itself, but the prosperity of manufacturing in large part determines the prosperity of other sectors. Agriculture benefits from the provision of chemicals and machinery, while displaced agricultural workers find better-paying factory jobs. Commercial services grow to satisfy the needs of industry and benefit from the technological innovations that industry provides, from railways to data processing. Growth of a successful manufacturing industry is *the* basis of national economic progress.

The criterion of economic success

But what does being 'successful' really amount to? In the market economy the criterion of success is the capture of markets. A successful manufacturing sector will dominate its home market, warding off attacks from abroad, and will sell enough output overseas to pay for the imports that are needed. Therefore a successful manufacturing sector is one that performs as well as, or better than, anyone else's manufacturing sector: it holds, or increases, its market share. By this criterion British manufacturing has been notably *un*successful since the war.

Since 1960 Britain's share of world trade in manufactures has fallen from 13 per cent of the market to only 7 per cent in 1980. Only the United States has done as badly, its share having fallen from 18 to 11 per cent.

Table 3. Shares of world exports of manufactures 1960-1980 (percentages)

	UK	US	W. Germany	France	Italy	Japan
1960	12.7	17.9	14.8	7.4	3.9	5.3
1970	8.6	15.3	15.8	6.9	5.7	9.3
1980	6.8	11.5	13.9	6.9	5.5	10.4

Sources: Cambridge Economic Policy Review, 1979
           National Institute Economic Review

Nor is it only in foreign markets that British industry has failed. At one time the label 'Made in Britain' was sufficient to attract the British customer away from goods bearing the demeaning title 'Foreign Made', but no longer. The dramatic examples of surrender in the home market, such as motor cycles, cars and televisions, are only the most visible catastrophes. From 1963 to 1980 the foreign share of the British market for manufactures has risen inexorably from 14.5 to 26 per cent. And the process is quickening. Half that loss of market occurred in the last seven years. These figures are the real substance of the British problem. (And of the American problem too. From 1963 to 1980 the foreign share of the American market tripled, rising from 2 per cent to 6.5 per cent. Half the increase has occurred in the last seven years.)

The riddle of 'competitiveness'

Why don't British manufactures sell, either at home or abroad? Why are they not, as they say, 'competitive'?

An immediate response might be: because they are too expensive, because British manufactures and British workers have simply priced themselves out of world markets. The evidence does not support this conclusion. Over the entire period in which Britain's share of world trade was halved, the average price of her manufactured exports showed no significant rise relative to that of her competitors'. If anything, it fell; only in 1979 and 1980 has there been any significant erosion of price competitiveness. This may surprise those who have been depressed by the regular assertion that over the years the competitiveness of British industry has been eroded by inflation. As we shall see, Britain's inflation record is not

Figure 2

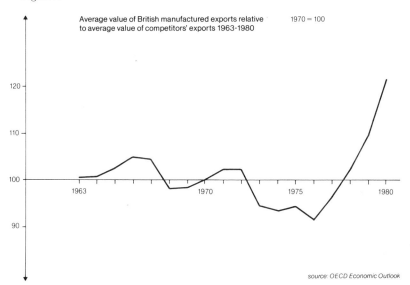

Average value of British manufactured exports relative to average value of competitors' exports 1963-1980   1970 = 100

source: OECD Economic Outlook

This index is based on changes in prices of exports, changes in exchange rates *and* Britain's pattern of trade. The competitors who have been taken into account are the United States, West Germany, France, Canada, Italy, the Netherlands, Sweden, Belgium, Switzerland, Austria, Denmark, Norway and Japan. An increase in the value of the index indicates a diminution of price competitiveness and vice versa.

The diagram shows that from 1963 to 1978 the largest fluctuation in British relative export prices was only of the order of 8 per cent – and that was downwards! The effect of the devaluation of 1967 can be seen to have been less long-lived than the effects of the general re-alignment of exchange rates in 1972. The latter was, of course, combined with a much tougher incomes policy (see the figure on p. 119). The deterioration of price competitiveness in the years 1979-1980 was brought about primarily by the very high value of the pound.

outstandingly bad vis-à-vis her competitors; and this, combined with changes in the rate of exchange between the pound and rival currencies, has been sufficient to keep British manufactures competitive in terms of price. None the less fewer and fewer people at home and abroad want to buy them.

Many attempts have been made to solve the riddle of competitiveness, and the answers all point in the same direction: prices are important in determining the pattern of trade, but they are far less important than many other factors. Among these are product design, intrinsic quality deriving from more advanced engineering techniques, reliability, servicing facilities and prompt delivery. These are the factors which explain the success of Sony televisions and Volkswagen cars in markets in which competing products are often significantly cheaper. But non-price factors are even more important in markets for machines and other manufactured inputs. The user of the more advanced machine has a great advantage over his less well-equipped rivals. In a sense, of course, 'you get what you pay for' – higher price is more than compensated by higher quality. The real question then is: Why is the quality of British goods so poor?

Productivity growth

'Quality' is an elusive attribute, made up as it is of many elements, ranging from better engineering techniques to a more efficient servicing network. Nevertheless some clue as to why one country's manufacturing sector performs better than another may be found in the fact that all these nonprice phenomena seem to go hand-in-hand with the rate of growth of output per worker employed in manufacturing, i.e. productivity growth. In those countries in which the rate of growth of output per worker is relatively high, products are better designed, better produced, better marketed and better serviced. High productivity growth may also help to keep prices low. But its most important benefits are the non-price improvements. A high rate of productivity growth is *the* determinant of a competitive manufacturing industry. Here is the key to our riddle, but the answer is still elusive. What will ensure that the rate of productivity growth is high enough to maintain the competitiveness of British manufacturing?

The determination of productivity growth

It is striking fact that productivity growth is a national phenomenon, a characteristic of the whole of the manufacturing sector of a country, rather than of individual industries. The country with the highest rate of productivity growth in manufacturing as a whole will tend to have the highest rate of productivity growth in individual industries also. In the early sixties Japan had the highest rate of productivity growth of the top seven industrial countries in textiles, chemicals, non-electrical machinery, electrical machinery, transport equipment and so on. France was number two or three in all these sectors, while Britain and the United States brought up the rear. The same overall picture may be seen in the early seventies. Japan remains number one in all sectors, with second place now held across the board by Germany. The United States has improved to about fourth place in all industries, but Britain is still firmly ensconced in last place.

If growth of output per head in manufacturing is a national phenomenon, the key to the riddle of competitiveness must be found in the determinants of the performance of the manufacturing sector as a whole, rather than in the achievements of individual firms or industries. A successful firm in an unsuccessful country will eventually be dragged down to the level of its compatriots.

The determinants of technical change, of the growth of output per worker, were the classical economists' fundamental concern, for these are the major determinants of the wealth of the nation.

The division of labour

Adam Smith had subsumed all the technical and social aspects of changing output per worker under the general heading of the 'division of labour'. The division of labour referred not only to the organisation of a factory, but to stages in the historical evolution of society – societies with little division of labour were more backward than societies in which tasks were more divided. But whichever aspect was considered, increasing division of labour meant increasing output per worker.

The division of labour, Adam Smith argued, was limited by the extent of the market and determined by the accumulation of stock – by which he meant the building of factories, the construction of machines and the development of roads and canals: the means of production and the means of extending the market.

Adam Smith did not make much progress in explaining the factors determining the accumulation of stock. This Ricardo attempted to do by a class analysis of spending. By elucidating what determined the distribution of income, especially what determined profits, he could analyse the accumulation of stock – for profits, it was assumed, were invested.

The labour process

Marx carried the story a stage further by a careful dissection of the forces bearing on the organisation of work – which he referred to as 'the labour process'. He emphasised the fact that work was a social process, which requires social discipline enforced by persuasion and compulsion. The prospect of promotion may be as great an incentive to hard work as the prospect of the sack. Technical innovation can play an important disciplinary role. The speed at which a machine operates, or at which a production line is run, will exert as much, perhaps even more, disciplinary power as the exhortations of manager.

There the discussion rested for eighty years. The neo-classical economists who took over economics at the end of the nineteenth century were not interested in the complex ramifications of growth and change. They were intent instead on showing that the self-adjusting market ensured an efficient allocation of scarce resources.

Productivity and the growth of demand

Keynes was another matter altogether. For Keynes's idea that the level of output and employment was determined by the level of demand led naturally to the idea that the growth of output and growth of employment were determined by the growth of demand. All that was needed was to link this insight to the classical discussion of technical change, and a new general theory of growth, technical progress and competitiveness – the analytical key to prosperity and depression in the modern world – was there for the asking.

It all seems obvious in retrospect. For, like all important new propositions, the central idea is simple – once somebody has it. The idea was Nicholas Kaldor's. In a study of growth in Western economies since the war, from which he hoped to draw lessons for the U.K., Kaldor (1908-) argued that the rate of growth of a modern economy is fundamentally determined by the rate of growth of output per worker in manufacturing, and that this, in turn, is determined by the rate of growth of demand for manufactures. In these two straightforward propositions, Kaldor synthesised the central insights of the classical economists and of Keynes, and verified the peculiar role of manufacturing. He also made clear why productivity growth is a characteristic of manufacturing as a whole. As a particular manufacturing industry grows, its operations can be broken down into a number of specialist activities. This division of labour both increases output per worker in that industry and spills over into other industries. A new specialist toolmaker, for example, may as well provide tools for the motor trade as for textile machinery. So, in a modern industrial country, all sectors are closely linked to each other. One industry's output is another industry's input, and their destinies cannot be separated.

Growth of demand for manufactures may come from growth either of the home or of the overseas market. In most countries it is the growth of the home market which is the major factor, for not only is the home market by far the dominant element in total demand – typically 80 per cent or more of the output of manufacturing industry is sold at home – but foreign markets are, by definition, less easy to manipulate. A country which relies heavily on export demand to maintain its rate of growth is likely to be dangerously exposed to the slings and arrows of world-market fortunes. So, although a high rate of growth of export demand can be a major stimulus, a high level of foreign trade is no guarantee of success. Of Britain's total domestic production from all industries, 18 per cent comprises exports of manufactures. The corresponding figure for Japan is only 9 per cent.

Cumulative causation

The key to solving our riddle and understanding the competitive dynamism of manufacturing is now in our grasp. High growth of demand gives productivity growth which, via price and non-price factors, gives competitive success, which in turn gives high growth of demand, which gives productivity, which gives competitiveness –

and so on and so on. This is the principle of cumulative causation.

The system clearly can work in reverse too. Low growth of demand gives low productivity growth, which gives competitive failure, which gives low growth of demand, which gives low productivity growth ... downhill all the way. A country which grows relatively slowly will see its relative position decline as others capture its markets at home and abroad. In the market system zero growth, however ecologically desirable, is impossible. For zero growth begets low productivity growth and so erodes the competitive position of industry until demand falls away completely and zero becomes negative: a recipe for clean air and human misery.

Degenerate productivity growth

When demand for manufactures ceases to grow, productivity may still rise as old factories are shut down – even though no new ones are built. Suppose, for example, that the whole of British industry were shut down apart from the Fawley oil refinery on Southampton Water where the value of the output of refined products per worker is enormous. At a stroke output per worker employed (and there wouldn't be many workers) would rise more rapidly than anywhere in the world. Then it would stop rising, for there would be no other factories left to close. Reducing the number of workers on out-of-date machines yields similarly limited productivity gains. This degenerate productivity growth occurs in most slumps and is just what has happened to British industry over the past couple of years, as large sections of British manufacturing have been closed. It is the swansong of a dying industry. Britain may be the best in the world at producing Rolls-Royces, but this will hardly be much good in the battle with Volkswagen, Renault and Datsun.

It is one of the enduring fallacies of economics, shared by economists of left and right alike, that market economies are revitalised by a slump to emerge 'leaner and fitter'. Lean certainly, fit perhaps – fit, and out of date. Reconstruction, which requires investment, takes place in a boom. It is the dynamic of growing economies that ensures true productivity growth. In the market economy the principle of cumulative causation ensures that success breeds success and failure breeds failure.

The institutional foundations of growth

But if cumulative causation is so powerful, why is success not perpetual? Why, if Britain was the most successful economy of the early nineteenth century, did she not remain a world leader?

Any pattern of economic development sets up institutions, social organisations and social philosophies which reflect the conflicts that economic change involves. As much as anything, major economic change requires the unifying excitement of emotional drama – the nationalism of Germany, the heroic frontier in the United States, the idea of modernisation in late-nineteenth-century Russia and, of course, the mission of Empire ... and free trade.

The excitement of Britain's economic and political leadership of the world was the excitement of a society throwing off the constraints of childhood and rushing eagerly into liberal adolescence. King Cotton ruled, and his court was in Manchester. A new group of philosophers, economists and politicians coalesced into the Manchester School – the intellectual symbol of liberalism, laissez faire and free trade. The British commitment to free trade was the fraternal twin of industrial success.

The new British industrial system of the nineteenth century was borne forward by the worldwide demand for its basic products, textiles and iron, a trade financed by the City of London. Britain was the only major country in which foreign demand played such an important role in industrialisation. For many years Britain was the only country producing manufactured goods in any substantial quantity. International trade meant trading with Britain. At the hub of the system the empire of British manufacturing was fuelled by the financial resources and organising skills of the City of London.

The City and free trade

The relics of this era are still apparent. The City of London remains perhaps the major international centre for the organisation of trade and finance. There are the world markets for commodites such as tin, copper and gold, for insurance and, most important of all, for money.

Typical of these markets is the Baltic Exchange. The Baltic Exchange is the major market in the world for one of the key elements in all international trade – space on ships. Like most of the important trading centres in the City of London, the Baltic Exchange grew out of one of the old coffee houses where brokers would gather to combine refreshment and business. For the Baltic it was the Virginia and Maryland Coffee House, later renamed the 'Virginia and Baltic' as its business diversified eastwards. Today 60 per cent of all the cargo space on the world's tramp ships is handled at one time or another by members of the Baltic Exchange.

The prosperity of the City is intimately linked to free trade – in the case of the Baltic Exchange, free trade in space on ships. The operations of the Baltic depend on freedom from national legislation requiring that goods be carried in ships of a particular country.

The peculiar character of Britain's industrialisation stamped a commitment to free trade on the British body politic as the hallmark of economic success. Nowhere is this commitment greater than in the financial and trading centres of the City of London. For the essence of successful financial operations is that money be able to flow in search of profit where it will, without let or hindrance.

The extent of this free market commitment has reached quite bizarre levels. For example, during the Crimean war Russian bonds, floated in Amsterdam, were financed indirectly by the London money market. When the propriety of dealing in the bonds of the enemy was debated in the House of Commons, Sir Thomas Baring argued that to introduce special measures as circumstances arose was not the way to legislate on a subject affecting trade; nor ought the Commons to be influenced by hostility or spite against a particular country in the enactment of such laws. *The Times* could only deplore legislation which banned any dealing connected with Russian bonds as the abandonment of 'the nicest matters of finance … to the headlong direction of popular passion'.

The beginnings of decline

At the time these words were written, and as Gladstone was perfecting the political economy of free trade and laissez faire, Britain's decline from pre-eminence as a manufacturing power was already well under way. In part this was due simply to the inevitable effect of other countries industrialising – a catching-up process which occupied the mid-years of the nineteenth century. But after about 1870 a more disturbing phenomenon made its appearance: Britain began to fall behind, not just in a few specialised lines, but in the bedrock industries – iron and steel, chemicals, heavy engineering and the source of power, electricity. Only in textiles was some dominance retained, and even in that industry which, more than any other, symbolised British industrialisation, the Japanese made heavy inroads into the Far East market.

The case of steel is particularly striking. All the great inventions of the steel age were British, from the Bessemer convertor of 1856, which ushered in the age of steel, to the Gilchrist-Thomas process of 1877-9, which permitted the use of cheap phosphoric ores, thereby cutting the price of steel by half and dealing a final blow to the mass use of wrought-iron.

But it was in Germany and the United States that the age of steel was truly born. In 1870 the average British open-hearth furnace was roughly the same size as a furnace in Germany. Twenty years later German furnaces were 50 per cent bigger and total production was 65 per cent greater. By 1900 steel production in the United States was four times greater than in Britain. Moreover the very size of German and American plants demanded mechanisation. The system of continuous rolling had been invented in Britain in the 1860s but it was not taken up. In the 1890s it was introduced on a large scale in the United States, and it was then adopted and perfected by German companies.

A yet more dramatic shift in industrial dominance occurred in the chemical industry, particularly in organic chemistry. Textiles require dyes. Natural dyes such as indigo or cochineal (which is made from the dried remains of a female beetle and is the basis of hunting pink dye) were therefore brought from the Empire. But their colour range was limited and quality control was haphazard. The key breakthrough was Perkin's accidental discovery of mauvine, a synthetic aniline dye, in 1856. Synthetic dyes would allow a wide range of colours and precise quality control. They were a British invention, but they were taken up in Germany. By the mid-1870s 50 per cent of the world market in synthetic dyes was controlled by German companies, and by the turn of the century 90 per cent. When war broke out in 1914 the British dye industry was in such severe straits that special Royal licences were issued to permit the purchase of khaki dye produced in Germany, notwithstanding the general prohibition against trading with the enemy. Synthetic dyes heralded the foundation of the organic chemical industry, which was later to encompass plastics and artificial fibres.

The same story is repeated over and over again. Applications of the new energy source, electricity, were seen in Britain as being severely limited. In 1894 the president of the British Institute of Mechanical Engineers stated that the chief purpose of public generating plants was, and probably always would be, to supply energy for lighting purposes. Power came from steam. Britain had built the railways of the world, but when large-scale electrification of the London underground railway was undertaken in 1905 the backward state of British electrical engineering was starkly revealed. Development of the deep tube system required three major innovations – tunnelling, electric traction and electric lifts. Tunnelling techniques had been perfected by Brunel and did not involve any major new development in manufacturing industry. Electric traction had also been pioneered in Britain, but it was developed in America and Germany. Indeed it was an American financier, Charles Yerkes, who was the driving force behind the 1905 electrification in London. The teams of workers were led by American engineers, and the carriages on the new lines were of French, American and even Hungarian manufacture. The electric lifts were also of American design, built in Britain by a subsidiary of the American Otis company.

In machine tools and precision engineering, and the standardisation of parts that this involved, Germany and America took the lead. In size of plant, standardisation of work practices, quality control and sheer innovation, Britain fell further and further behind. British was not often cheapest and seldom best.

The reasons for Britain's dramatic loss of leadership have been hotly debated for a hundred years, but our analysis of the determinants of success in manufacturing industry provides some important clues.

New institutions

The challenge of early British success had forced other countries to adopt new strategies to ensure a high rate of growth of demand for their domestic industry. New institutional arrangements were required to launch industries on a scale that could compete with the British, and to protect home markets for those industries against British competition. So in France, Germany, Russia, Japan and the United States economic institutions were forged which were fundamentally different from those in Britain and remain fundamentally different in many respects to the present day.

In all those countries, in sharp contrast to Britain, an active role was played by the state in promoting industrialisation. The most important state activity required the abandonment not only of laissez faire, but of free trade too. By protecting and subsidising domestic industry the state sought to overcome the disadvantages of initial backwardness. In 1904 the average level of tariffs on industrial products imported from Britain was 25 per cent in Germany, 34 per cent in France, 73 per cent in the United States and 131 per cent in Russia. The British tariff on manufactured imports was zero.

Governments also intervened directly in the drive to industrialise, setting up companies where necessary and importing foreign technicians and businessmen to run them. Eric Hobsbawm has noted that Britain was the only country which systematically refused any fiscal protection to its industries, and the only country in which government neither built, not helped to finance (directly or indirectly), or even planned, any part of the railway system.

New financial institutions were also needed in other countries to overcome British industrial dominance. In France, Germany, and the United States the banks were organised for the express purpose of promoting industrialisation, mobilising the mass of small savings in the service of heavy industries. Close links were forged between the banks and industrial enterprise. In Britain the banks were devices for investing the fortunes of the well-off in trade ventures and government bonds. German banks were founded for people who needed money, whereas British banks were for people who had money.

Industry and finance

In Britain the interests of industry and the interests of finance have never been as closely intertwined as they are in France, Germany were in the United States. As the decline of British manufacturing became evident, the competitive strength of foreign industry weakened somewhat the enthusiasm for free trade previously displayed by British manufacturers, but British financiers were still doing well out of financing the trade of the world. When, at the turn of the century, Joseph Chamberlain tried to rally the manufacturing interest in the Conservative Party behind the cause of protection for domestic industry, in the hope of launching a manufacturing revival, he was bitterly opposed by the financial interests. He and the manufacturers were decisively defeated.

The full extent of the victory of finance was to be demonstrated much later, in 1925, after the First World War had finally destroyed the edifice of British economic superiority. During the war normal free financial relations had been suspended. In particular, Britain had abandoned the gold standard, which had been the basis of the international monetary system guided from London. At the end of the war the City, in the interests of sound finance and the restoration of its position as an international financial centre, pressed the Chancellor of the Exchequer, Winston Churchill, to return to the gold standard, even though this would mean raising the value of the pound against the dollar and damaging the competitiveness of the export industries. Again the victory was won by finance, in the person of Montague Norman, Governor of the Bank of England; and the gold standard was restored.

In a bitter polemical pamphlet entitled *The Economic Consequences of Mr Winston Churchill*, Keynes argued that this decision would lead to disaster. He was right. The export industries – coal, shipbuilding, textiles – virtually collapsed. In 1926 there was a General Strike. Britain's slump was well under way five years before the depression was to engulf the rest of the world.

The end of economic dominance

The collapse of the late twenties was the culmination of a bitter competitive struggle which for sixty years had pitted British laissez faire against the continental weapon of state-protected, bank-financed industrialisation.

Laissez faire lost.

Laissez faire lost because the market system creates a vital contradiction between the interests of individual firms and the interests of the economy as a whole. If firms have sunk their capital in equipment and factories which produce goods which can still be sold somewhere, the incentive to scrap perfectly good equipment in the interests of modernisation is rather weak. If all firms could be organised into a modernisation drive, they would provide the demand for each other's products and would all be better off. But in a competitive economy organised only by the market, the uncertainty of demand and the cost involved in a large-scale re-equipment may well outweigh potential profits – even if the finance can be found from meagre current profits and an uninterested banking system.

The vital factor in the defeat was the relatively slow growth of demand for British goods at home and abroad. Locked out of the fast-growing American and European markets, the British sold their increasingly outdated goods in less dynamic Imperial markets. In 1913 Argentina and India bought more iron and steel from Britain than did the whole of Europe. Cut off from the fast-growing markets enjoyed by their competitors, British manufacturers didn't stand a chance.

The ground lost in the late nineteenth century has never been fully recovered. The brief periods in which Britain has appeared to be catching up have been stifled before maturity was reached – stifled, as much as anything, by her institutional and intellectual heritage: a commitment to ideas and to ways of doing things that are erroneous and irrelevant.

In a market system countries which fail to keep pace fall by the wayside. Not only do standards of living rise more slowly, but it becomes more and more difficult to maintain full employment even at those lower standards of living. If institutional reform does not limit and redirect the working of the market, the principle of cumulative causation will grind the weak economy down.

The market system is peculiarly inflexible when faced with long-term economic changes. Without some form of guiding hand, industrial systems seem to ossify. The institutions and ideas that were the basis of success become the fetters on the future. Nowhere is this more apparent than in Britain, where it has not been possible to find the combination of ideas and institutions which would ensure the high rate of growth of demand for manufactured output which is the prerequisite of successful development and, ultimately, of the maintenance of full employment in a competitive world.

4

The Keynesian Ideology

The power of the market may be controlled, if it can be controlled at all, only by the power of the state. But British success was based on free trade and laissez faire which meant a government abdication of economic power to the market. Government economic activity grew in nineteenth-century Britain but did not impinge on the market organisation of production. In France and Germany the role of the state was quite different. In France through centralised authority, and in Germany via the power of the industrial banks, the state played a major role in economic organisation. Keynesian ideas on economic management seemed to herald a new era of state intervention in Britain. But Keynes's views were formed into a new Keynesian Ideology which limited the role of the government to the overall management of demand, leaving industrial structure and the composition of investment to the market. The Keynesian Ideology preserved free-market economics as a fundamental premise of British economic policy.

* * *

So far I have portrayed economic life in a market economy as if every single aspect of it were organised through markets by purchase and sale. This has helped in the identification of some crucial elements in the way the system works, and in the way people think it works. But as a picture of any economy, let alone of the economy of modern Britain, it is clearly seriously inaccurate.

A considerable amount of economic activity is not organised through the market. Within the family goods and services are produced and distributed according to rules other than the grim calculation of profit and loss. The Sunday-morning deal made with the children to induce them to wash the car is less an example of economic calculation than a means of salving the conscience of parents who prefer to stay in bed and read the Sunday newspapers. Bonds of affection, traditional and accepted division of tasks, and not a little economic planning direct the economic activities of the household.

This unconquered arena has proved attractive to the market. Where commodities are produced and consumed, they can be produced and sold for profit. Nor has the market alone penetrated family life: the neo-classical economists have too. They have taken their vision of economic man as a rational, utility-maximising being trading in the market place and thrust it into the privacy of the home. A 'theory of marriage' has been developed which characterises matrimony as just another calculation of profit and loss, the full details of which are too delicate for these pages. Sadly, the conclusions of these dissections of human behaviour tend to be rather trite. In a recent analysis of the economics of extra-marital affairs, it was shown that the greatest number of affairs will be enjoyed by those who have the most free time.

Although there is a wide range of economic tasks organised within the family according to non-market rules, the family's activities are closely hemmed in by the market. To survive, the family must sell and buy. The market is the ultimate arbiter of its fate.

The economic role of the state

The government, while often pretending that its role is equivalent to managing the family budget of the nation, in fact has much greater scope to pursue non-market strategies. Indeed it can, in principle, banish the market and try to organise economic life in other ways. But whether it plays an active role in economic affairs or passively hands over the economy to the market, the state is clearly a key economic institution. Active state policies were, as we have seen, an important element in the industrialisation of all countries other than Britain. In reasonably favourable circumstances an active government policy, such as was pursued in Germany, France or the United States, may be able to discipline the market and point the principle of cumulative causation in a favourable direction. Therefore our neglect so far of the role of state institutions has been an important omission in our overall picture of the market system and Britain.

The development of the liberal economy was accompanied by the development of a liberal polity. The actions of the state were now to be expressions of the will of all its citizens – an image of the state directed by the decisions of individuals in the same way as the decisions of individuals are the determining factors in the liberal image of the market. The later growth of bureaucracy, corporate and union, in the running of the economy, has likewise been reflected in the development of a more bureaucratic state apparatus. The vexed question as to whom, if anyone, this apparatus represents is not really an element in our story. But we should remember that the state, like other social institutions, embodies the ideologies and prejudices of the past and the present, which, it will argue, are 'in the national interest' – of which it is the supreme representative.

In Adam Smith's blueprint for the new market system the role of the state was strictly limited. If markets were to liberate the forces of economic growth and modernisation, to permit the increased specialisation and division of labour which are the basis of the wealth of the nation, then all the old Elizabethan apparatus of state control must be swept away. There must be freedom in the markets for goods, including foreign markets and foreign goods, and there must be freedom in the market for labour.

This did not mean that the state must fade away. Almost a quarter of the *Wealth of Nations* is devoted to a detailed study of the proper organisation of the economic activities of government. There were still important 'expenses of the sovereign' to be met by an efficient system of taxation: the defence of the realm and the provision of a system of law and order – notably for the enforcement of property rights. Then there were the 'expenses of public Works and Institutions for facilitating the Commerce of the Society', 'the expense of the Institutions for the Education of Youth' and 'of People of all Ages'; and last, though by no means least, there was 'the Expense of supporting the Dignity of the Sovereign'.

While performing all these tasks, the state should leave the market to handle the economic affairs of the country.

Laissez faire

The concept of a laissez-faire economy covers a wide range of different levels of government intervention in the workings of the economy – from an economy in which the role of the government is at the absolute minimum necessary to merit the name and taxing and spending hardly impinge on the private sector, to an economy in which the state plays a major part in providing the framework of health, education, roads and so on required for the private sector to operate satisfactorily. The crucial point is that all activities which can be performed by private industry are performed by the private sector. As far as trade is concerned, the term 'free trade' may encompass a similar range of state activity. Trade is unlikely to be totally 'free'. The nineteenth-century free-trading British state took considerable pains to manipulate and direct the trade of Empire.

All in all it was a vision of the rational laissez faire state that was to dominate nineteenth-century thinking. The social, political and economic beliefs of the new manufacturing classes were most vividly embodied in the person of W.E. Gladstone – the very symbol of 'national liberty', laissez faire and free trade. By 1874 Gladstone had reduced the role of government to so minimal a level that he could propose abolishing income tax, then 2d in the pound – less than 1 per cent.

Social policy

But the role of the state did not go on shrinking. Indeed by the 1870s the tide was already running strongly in the opposite direction. After all, the government was charged with the responsibility of providing an environment in which industry might prosper. The horrors of the early stages of industrialisation – the appalling squalor of Manchester and the other new industrial towns, the vicious exploitation of children in the factories, the human degradation on which the new wealth and power of Britain was built – all this must be mitigated by legislation lest it inspire revulsion against the system as a whole. Thus the Factory Acts and Mines Acts and the extraordinarily wide-ranging and perceptive activities of Factory Inspectors and Commissioners were a response to the workings of the market system. Though aimed at constraining the market to some degree, they were ultimately necessary for its acceptance and survival.

Moreover, as the complexity of industrial life increased, so education was necessary if the labour force was to be adequate to the demands placed upon it. The Education Act of 1870 provided for universal primary education, though the reform of higher education, still largely seen as irrelevant to the needs of British industry, was to come much later. The health of the working classes was of less concern, until the rejection as medically unfit of 25 per cent of potential recruits for the Boer War – and standards were not notably high – alerted the authorities to the appalling state of health in the country as a whole.

The momentum of intervention in the market in the interests of social welfare was reinforced by the growth in Britain and elsewhere of an increasingly self-confident labour movement. Bismarck's social-insurance schemes in the 1880s, like Lloyd George's unemployment insurance in 1911, were a reaction to pressure by working-class groups.

But despite the growing role of the state in factory legislation, health and education, and even in unemployment pay, the basic economic doctrine remained the same: the management of the British economy could be safely left to the market. The government might play an important role in balancing and defusing social conflicts, and even in providing some necessary services to industry, some education and some roads; but laissez faire and free trade were the enduring twin pillars of British success.

Other countries were interested, even envious, but not convinced. The obvious economic success of Britain, and the combination of liberal economics with increasing political freedom was an attractive mixture. But in France, Germany and the United States there was suspicion of Britain's eager advocacy of the other pillar of her programme, free trade. In the first half of the nineteenth century these countries' fledgling manufacturing companies could not hope to compete with the Midlands and Lancashire. If they were to catch up, new institutions and new policies must be devised.

The critique of free trade

Economists are not the sort of people to whom, as a rule, public monuments are erected. Yet one of the main squares in the town of Reutlingen in the West German Land of Baden-Württemberg is named after the economist whose statue stands in its centre. The paradox is heightened by the fact that the man so honoured by the town of his birth, and by the naming in his memory of squares and streets all over Germany, was an economist of whom most people in Britain have never heard. He was Friedrich List (1789-1846). It was

List who made the intellectual case against free trade, and his ideas were to be a major influence on German economic policy.

As a young man List first worked as a local administrator in the Town Hall at Tübingen. He rose rapidly in the civil service of the state of Württemberg to beome a ministerial under-secretary. At the age of 27 he was appointed to the newly created Chair of Political Economy at the University of Tübingen, an appointment he was unable to hold for long because of the unpopularity of his views on German unification.

List's analyses of the problems facing Germany in its attempt to industrialise were most comprehensively presented in his book *The National System of Political Economy*, published in 1841. List argued that Britain's commitment to, and advocacy of, free trade was simply a device for maintaining British economic dominance. British condemnation of state interference in economic affairs was dismissed as pure hypocrisy.

List insisted that the industrial revolution in Britain had been born not of free trade, but of protection – and protection, as he put it, of the most overt and political kind. The successful development of the cotton industry in Lancashire had first required the suppression of the Indian textile industry:

> Had they sanctioned the free importation into England of Indian cotton and silk goods [List wrote], the English cotton and silk manufactories must of necessity come to a stand. India had not only the advantage of cheaper labour and raw materials, but also the experience, the skill and the practice of centuries. The effect of these advantages could not fail to tell under a system of free competition. But England was unwilling to found settlements in Asia in order to become subservient to Asia in manufacturing industry ... Accordingly England prohibited the import of Indian cotton. The prohibition was complete and preremptory.

The Indians were not the only victims of British interference in the colonial manufacturing trade in the interests of home producers. Many lines of manufacturing, including the production of horse-shoe nails, were prohibited in the American colonies in order to encourage imports from Britain. List catalogued example after example of British commercial manipulation: in the colonies, in Portugal, in France, in Latin America – wherever sufficient political pressure could be exerted. The enthusiasm for free trade came only after Britain had achieved a dominant position in manufacturing:

> It is a very common clever device [List argued] that when
> anyone has attained the summit of greatness he kicks away the
> ladder by which he has climbed up in order to deprive others
> of the means of climbing up after him. In this lies the secret of
> the cosmopolitical doctrine of Adam Smith, and of the
> cosmopolitical tendencies of his great contemporary, William
> Pitt.
>
> Any nation which by means of protective duties and
> restriction on navigation has raised her manufacturing power
> and her navigation to such a degree of development that no
> other nation could sustain free competition with her can do
> nothing wiser than to throw away these ladders of her
> greatness, to preach to other nations that she has hitherto
> wandered in the paths of error and has now, for the first time,
> succeeded in discovering the truth.

List's ideas rapidly became influential in Germany, where they were
in accord with the new political climate. They validated and
reinforced the protectionist strategies of the German customs union,
the *Zollverein*, and were later to provide much of the intellectual
underpinning of Bismarck's national economic policies. List had not
denied that market freedom could stimulate accumulation. Indeed
he argued vigorously for the unification of Germany to create the
large internal market in which German industry might thrive. But
what was absolutely necessary was that domestic manufacturers
should be protected against foreign competition. Only then could
the full power of manufacturing be developed. And what was good
for manufacturing was good for other sectors too. The economic
health of agriculture and commerce depended on the economic
health of manufacturing.

Economists who believe in the efficiency of free markets and
particularly of free trade, having been forced to acknowledge the
strength of List's arguments, have sought to categorise them as
applying only to countries with 'infant industries'. When these
industries grow up to achieve equality with leading countries, free
trade should be the rule. What advocates of this position have failed
to notice is that the protecting countries forged ahead of Britain.
The dynamic benefits of high growth of demand guaranteed by
protection apparently far outweighted the inefficiencies, if any, of
the protection policies.

American policies

List's ideas also fell on fertile soil outside Germany. After his failure to retain the chair at Tübingen, List left Württemberg and travelled for some years in the United States, where he became a personal friend both of Andrew Jackson and James Madison. His first major publication attacking free trade and advocating protection of national industry was his *Outlines of American Political Economy*, which appeared in Philadelphia in 1827 and was published under the auspices of the Pennsylvania Society for the Promotion of Manufactures and the Mechanic Arts. America wholeheartedly embraced protection with the general tariff of 1828.

The French view of the state

In France, too, List's ideas were warmly received. The ground had been well prepared. Indeed List himself had claimed that he was simply repeating the views of Jean-Baptiste Colbert (1619-1683). Colbert had been a brilliant finance minister under Louis XIV who tried to stimulate French manufacturing by centralising the organisation of production and strictly prohibiting imports. Adam Smith dismissed Colbert as 'a laborious and plodding man of business'. List argued that with Colbert the 'palmy days of French industry began'.

Colbert's views on the need to centralise, control and direct, which were embodied in the institutional structure of France by Napoleon's political reforms, have provided the keynote of French economic policy for the past two hundred years, with but a few aberrant and much-regretted lapses.

But it is not only the centralisation of economic institutions which has been inherited from the time of Colbert. Much modern French economic thinking retains the Colbertian doctrine that it is quality rather than price that will be decisive in trade. This is a view which is remarkably in tune with the modern world, in which technically sophisticated products are likely to acquire market dominance. And it is considerably at variance with the traditional British concern with price. As Andrew Schonfield put it, it is a contrast between the views of producer and shopkeeper.

The impulse to control is still evident today. The Common Market is an organisation which decrees that most powers of economic control be surrendered to the forces of the market. But not only did the French play a major role in fixing the rules of the Common Market; they have never hesitated to bend the rules when the interests of France are at stake. There is in France an ingrained distrust of the workings of the free market, and a profound conviction that central direction by a small number of able persons is greatly superior to the haphazard uncertainties of the market.

Planning

That small number can be as small as twenty-five. A modest but elegant building in a quiet Parisian side street today houses the *Commissariat Général du Plan*, where just twenty-five persons attempt to plan the economic destiny of France. The *Commissariat* is just one of the many institutions in which are embodied the French centralising view of economic affairs, but it is one of the most important. For since the Second World War it has been the job of the *Commissariat*, together with other elements in the government machine, to persuade, enforce and direct the industrial reconstruction of France. To this end it possesses what to the British seem quite extraordinary powers. It can direct credit, vary taxes, raise or lower protective duties. It has even used mechanisms of price control set up as part of a government anti-inflation policy for the quite different task of deliberately driving small firms out of business, leaving only the large firms, which are easier to deal with. All this in the interest of a coherent economic policy.

The control which the *Commissariat Général* and other government agencies can exert over the operation of the French economy is greatly enhanced by two major characteristics of French economic life.

First, the participation of the government in the operations of manufacturing industry is far greater than in most other western countries. Nationalisation, either total or partial, has been used as a device for stimulating modernisation and change. The nationalised Renault car company, for example, has lead the French motor-car industry into an extremely powerful position in the world market. Then there are the many *enterprises mixtes*, part government, part privately owned and strongly government influenced, which have been used as the pace-setters in many industries, introducing new products, techniques and methods of organisation.

Secondly, the *Commissariat* can influence the development of all French industry by the control it exerts over finance. All the major

French banks have been nationalised since the war, and recently even the smaller, more specialised banks have been taken into public ownership. But more important than public ownership have been the elaborate mechanisms which give the French government, and its agent, the *Commissariat*, the power to vet all major financial transactions and guide flows of credit in accordance with government plans. Public control of the levers of finance has given the *Commissariat* access to an enormous amount of information the government would not otherwise possess, and the means to use it. French firms have learnt it is just not worth asking their bank for a loan of any size without first clearing the deal with the *Commissariat*.

Industrial banking

This financial power is enhanced by the far more important role played by the French banks in the finance of industry than by their British counterparts. For whereas British banks grew on the financing of trade and government debt, the modern French banks were developed to provide finance for industry. France is the birthplace of the industrial bank, a form of financial institution that has played a vital role in the industrial growth of France, as it has of Germany.

The role of the industrial bank is to lend long, to provide long-term finance for new industrial projects – a task regarded by British bankers as financially dangerous. The British view seemed to be confirmed when the first great industrial bank, the *Crédit Mobilier*, established by the Pereire brothers, collapsed in 1857. This, however, was but the first faltering step in what was to become a dynamic, powerful institutional system.

The German banks

The concept of industrial banking was eagerly taken up in Germany as the answer to the problem of mobilising sufficient finance to build factories large enough to compete against the British. The German banks became the politico-economic agency for the creation of the German industrial state. In place of the system of central direction used in France, it was the great industrial banks that co-ordinated, directed and reformed manufacturing industry.

The long-term commitment of finance requires a close

relationship between lender and borrower: nothing develops mutual concern quite so much as the possibility of losing money. Therefore industrial banks in France and Germany are closely involved in the organisation and running of industry. In France this involvement is part of the elaborate apparatus of the state. In Germany it is formalised through a unique two-tier structure of corporate management. Every company has both a management board which handles the day-to-day running of the company, and an *Aufsichstrat*, or supervisory board, which plans the long-term strategy of the company. The *Aufsichtsrat* is made up of representatives of shareholders and of labour. But the key influence is the influence of the banks – more particularly of the big three banks, the Commerzbank, the Deutsche Bank and the Dresdner Bank, who between them hold more than half the places held by banks on the supervisory boards of German industrial companies. And the heads of the major industrial companies sit on the supervisory boards of the banks, completing the circle of mutual interest.

The largest bank in Germany, the Deutsche Bank, was founded by the great industrialist Georg von Siemens in 1870. Today the close relationship between the Bank and the industrial firm of Siemens continues. Directors of Siemens sit on the supervisory board of the Deutsche Bank and directors of the Deutsche Bank sit on the supervisory board of Siemens. There is a similar relation between the Deutsche Bank and the Mannesmann Company, one of the world's largest makers of steel pipes and tubes.

In 1890 the brothers Mannesmann invented a new process for making steel tubes. This process resulted in seamless tubes which could withstand much higher pressures than the traditional, seamed tubes. Unfortunately the brothers could not find financial support for their invention within the steel industry. They turned for advice to von Siemens, who referred them to his cousin who was a director of the Deutsche Bank. The Bank decided to support the new idea and assigned one of its own directors to aid in the establishment of the Mannesmann Company. The results were at first disastrous. Nevertheless the Bank maintained its support over the first fifteen difficult years until the company at last paid a dividend in 1906.

Long-term commitment and an interest in innovation are characteristic of the German banks to this day, as is their central role in industrial organisation. A leading German banker recently portrayed the banks as 'a force for intra-industry co-ordination and rationalisation'. In a country like Germany, in which the role of the stock market is very limited – indeed most industrial companies are not quoted on the German stock exchange – the banks are the key agents in financing investment and mergers.

The banks and the state

This high degree of co-ordination between industry and finance could be a major source of instability. The long loans to industry do place the capital of the banks at great risk, which no amount of regular attendance at supervisory board meetings can fully offset. Collapse of a major industrial company would place great strain on the financial system and could reverberate throughout the economy. Some overall direction is required.

The idea of detailed national control of economic affairs carries unpleasant echoes of the Nazi era, and so is uncompromisingly rejected in Germany today. But the impulse to centralise is deeply ingrained in the economic institutions of Germany. The concept of centralised political authority has been replaced by a theory of consensus. Between the banks, the big companies and their industry associations and the state everything works towards consensus. It is the accepted way of doing things. Most German industrialists and bankers are shocked by the idea that they operate anything other than a free-market system. As Andrew Shonfield put it, the German system is one of 'organised private enterprise'. The continuing dialogue creates *de facto* an extremely flexible system of economic organisation dedicated to a common objective, the industrial prosperity of Germany.

The close relationship which exists today between industry, the government and the banks in Germany derives from institutional arrangements developed in the nineteenth century, as does the centralised planning system in France. Both of these quite different ways of organising economic affairs evolved out of a need to constrain and direct the market. It cannot be emphasised too strongly that in France and Germany the idea that the efficient organisation of economic affairs can be left entirely to the impersonal forces of the market has never been accepted as it has in Britain. On the contrary, the market is but one element to be used in economic management, and where long-term structural change is concerned some form of centralised direction is required. The market cannot be trusted.

The end of laissez faire?

The nineteenth-century developments which laid the foundation of the modern economic institutions of France and Germany were in many ways a reaction to British economic success – a success bred not of central direction but of joyful and willing surrender to the embrace of laissez faire. Today, however, the nineteenth-century laissez-faire state seems to have vanished into history. In Britain the role of the government expanded significantly before the First World War, and it expanded again between the wars. Since 1945 it has grown enormously. Now the state permeates all aspects of economic life – and much of non-economic life too. There is the National Health Service, the welfare state and the education system. In industry there are major nationalised industries, state regulation of the location of industry, building regulations and so on. Then, on and off, we have foreign exchange controls and controls of hire purchase. In all these ways, and many more, the economic role of the state has mushroomed.

Well yes – and no!

The welfare state and its paraphernalia are really the outcome of the steady advance of social reform which began before the First World War. This advance reflects both the needs of an increasingly complex industrial system and the growth in political pressures in favour of socially provided goods and services. The welfare state is, fundamentally, the modern equivalent of the Poor Laws. It owes nothing to ideas of economic management or to Keynes.

Economic management

It was the Keynesian idea that the economy could be *managed* that created an entirely new role for the state in Britain. Keynes's argument that the market did not work to ensure full employment and that what was needed was action on investment led to the development of an elaborate theory of economic management. Indeed the theoretical perspective was so broad as to encompass a variety of 'tendencies', ranging from those who argued that the state should manipulate demand at one remove, by varying taxes and interest rates to stimulate or discourage spending, to those who saw in Keynes's writing the rudiments of a manifesto for a planned economy. In Britain the former tendency prevailed.

Keynes's description of how to manage the economy appeared to be amply confirmed by the experience of economic policy during the Second World War, which from Kingsley Wood's budget of 1941 onwards was run on Keynesian principles. Nor was this true only of Britain. In the United States the wartime administration of price control and industrial planning was firmly in the hands of young Keynesian economists. Moreover the pre-war success of Nazi economic policies further demonstrated that government action could achieve what markets could not – a demonstration that Keynes acknowledged in his preface to the 1936 German edition of his *General Theory*.

Since governments could now ensure full employment, they ought to ensure it. The opening sentence of the 1944 White Paper 'Employment Policy' affirmed that 'The Government accept as one of their primary aims and responsibilities the maintenance of a high and stable level of employment after the War'. This statement marked the most important change in the economic philosophy of the British government since the abolition of the Corn Laws.

The Keynesian Ideology

During the war the Treasury was captured by Keynesian economists, and Keynesian principles were to dominate thinking in government circles for the next twenty-five years or so. But Keynes's idea that markets do not work efficiently was really only accepted at one level – at the level of the overall operation of the economy, not at the level of individual industries. The job of the government was to maintain the aggregate level of employment by fixing interest rates, taxes and government expenditure at appropriate levels. The government might also be concerned with the general rate of inflation, and must take some action to keep the balance of payments in reasonable shape. Having looked after the broad perspective, it should leave the rest of economic life to the market. The market would handle it efficiently.

So the structure of industry, investment policies, the development of new products and new technologies, the very future of the economy, was handed back to the market. And there were plenty of economists around to argue that this was a Good Thing.

Thus was born the Keynesian Ideology – a new Treasury View to replace the discredited Treasury View of 1929: a grand new synthesis in which, paradoxically, Keynesian ideas were used to resuscitate and prop-up the free-market economics of Keynes's erstwhile opponents.

The Keynesian Ideology dominated British economic and political life for thirty years after the war and is still a powerful force. It was the economic element in the Butskellite consensus – that happy unity of principle embodied in the persons of R.A. Butler and Hugh Gaitskell which guided both Conservative and Labour governments.

In recent years the commitment to full employment has gone, to be replaced, perhaps temporarily, by the canons of monetarism. Monetarism rests on the belief that the market knows best – a belief that was easy to revive among economists and politicians who had never really abandoned it. The Keynesian Ideology has been an intellectual device to enable the free-market orthodoxy to survive after the humiliation of the 1930s.

There has, of course, been some government intervention in the detailed workings of the market. Regional policies which direct and persuade firms to locate in particular areas are an attempt to alleviate the conditions in regions which the market has condemned to depression and decay. Similarly, government rescues of beleaguered enterprises – Ferranti, Rolls Royce, British Leyland and so on – represent a refusal to accept fully the blinkered and remorseless logic of the market. These aspects of government economic policy are essentially defensive.

Not only have intervention and discrimination as a means of positive industrial planning not been practised in Britain – they have been regarded with distaste. The declaration that any economic policy is discriminatory is an act of condemnation. The Selective Employment Tax introduced by the Wilson government in the 1960s was attacked on just these grounds, even though the level of discrimination was only at the level of the broadest tripartite division between agriculture, industry and services. The French practice of varying the tax liability and manipulating the financial status of individual firms to enforce compliance with government objectives would be anathema in Britain.

The status of government economic activity is also notably low. It is a commonplace of economic debate that civil servants are incompetent when it comes to industrial matters. Their training, experience and education declare their unfitness for the nitty-gritty of restructuring industry, or even of running a firm. Nationalised companies are seen as the also-rans in the race for efficiency. In France nationalised firms and *enterprises mixtes* enjoy the prestige accorded industrial leaders in the more dynamic sectors of the economy. In Britain, by contrast, nationalisation has in many cases been a method of picking up the pieces, of reorganising rundown industry – a service of mercy to the fallen: always rather embarrassing, like a public display of grief.

Half-hearted planning

As a consequence of this timorous obeisance to the majesty of the market, planning in Britain has been notably half-hearted. Lacking any accepted intellectual justification, it has been based on the theory of 'indicative planning'. The basic idea of this theory is that the market would know best if only it could see a little further into the future. Planners can solve this problem by gathering information about the investment intentions of companies and estimating the spending intentions of individuals and then coordinating and publishing the results as an 'indication' to the market of what the future may be like. Apart from the fact that it is not at all obvious that firms in a competitive economy will be prepared to tell the whole truth and nothing but the truth concerning their future plans, the notion of 'indicative planning' elevates the exchange of information above the formulation of any conception of what is to be done.

So, while Britain has probably as many government institutions and agencies that are supposed to plan as any Western country, these have precious little power. George Brown's attempt to circumvent the Treasury and recreate the *Commissariat du Plan*, in the form of the Department of Economic Affairs, and its 1965 *National Plan* failed dismally, because it had no teeth. Lacking the French control levers of key firms in every industry and the vital control over finance, it was an exercise in wishful thinking. Soon the entire exercise was abandoned to short-term expediency. The reaction to the balance of payments crisis of July 1966 was yet another surrender to the power of the market. The *National Plan*, and with it any commitment, however slight, to long-term planning, was effectively abandoned.

Two lessons may be learned from this sad exercise.

First, the control of finance is an essential component of the successful restructuring of industry. The German banks have always worked closely with the state in securing the mutually agreed objective of industrial advance. In France the government controls credit directly. In Britain the allocation of finance is left to the market.

Secondly, a successful industrial policy requires long-term stability of purpose and practice. The fundamental difference between the economic organisation of Britain and her two great continental neighbours has been that in both France and Germany industrial policy has been conducted with a view to the long run, while in Britain the short run has dominated.

The Keynesian Ideology has resulted not only in a concern with full employment, which is all well and good, but in a preoccupation with the balance of payments and inflation – with short-run reaction to the market, rather than with long-run use of the market.

The role and influence of Keynesian ideas

Keynesian ideas have had significantly less influence in France and Germany than in Britain. But in both France and Germany the pursuit of policies of industrial reconstruction and development has involved the implementation of measures to ensure that the products of reconstructed industry are sold. The Germans call such policies 'supply-support' policies, which, roughly translated, means demand policies. By means of subsidies, government purchasing and, in France, protection from foreign competition, the long-term demand for individual industries is assured as best as may be. Government expenditure, in particular, has a distinct structural flavour. Demand is therefore maintained and manipulated at the level of the individual industry and is backed up by financial policies designed to provide long-term protection against the short-term vicissitudes of the market.

In Britain, where Keynes's ideas were embraced more enthusiastically than anywhere else, the result has been doubly perverse. Instead of establishing the need to control market forces, the status of the market has been revived. Instead of raising the question of the long-run development of the economy, the focus has been obsessively short-run.

The Keynesian Ideology provided a comforting blanket into which the ideas and prejudices of nineteenth-century Britain could snuggle. Keynes himself contributed to this effect. When some of the ramifications of his ideas were elaborated by his followers, he recoiled from their anti-market content and attempted to patch together a role for the market and a role for the state, Since there is clearly is a role for both, it was easy to slip into the view that the best role for the market was, with just a little modification, the role it had always played in Britain. More radical reforms to control and direct the market were unnecessary.

Perhaps the major paradox to be found in popular discussions of Britain's current plight is the widespread belief that the government interferes widely in the economy. In fact, where positive direction is concerned, the role of the government in Britain is significantly less than in France or Germany – indeed in any of our continental neighbours. Only in the United States is government action similarly frowned upon. The parallels that exist between British and American economic performance have already been noted.

But in the modern interdependent world economy, the powers of any government to control the economic destiny of its country are circumscribed by the international market. Like the family, the organisation of the internal affairs of the nation will be hemmed in by the need to sell to, and buy from, the world outside.

5

The Market on a World Scale

The international trading system has a major influence on the economic destiny of countries caught up in it. The old static analysis presents a harmonious view of trade. The principle of cumulative causation reveals trading relations to be anything but harmonious. Acting through the balance of payment positions of weak countries, it reinforces cumulative decline. Adjustments to the pattern of international trade by devaluation and deflation are generally unsuccessful. The prosperity of the world system therefore relies on the organising power of a Big Spender. In the absence of a Big Spender the world system has a fundamental deflationary basis. This is the case today.

* * *

The peculiarity of the social and economic organisation of the West today is that control of economic life has been abdicated to a system which, by its very nature, is uncontrollable. That 'peculiar institution' is the world market.

A world trading system has existed for centuries, but the modern system in which production is linked on a world scale is part of the great British invention. The development of manufacturing industry demanded a new form of trading relationship. Since industry needs both raw materials and markets, a two-way trade grew rapidly between raw material suppliers and the new manufacturing nations.

But it did not grow as rapidly as trade between the manufacturing nations themselves. It is this trade between industrial countries which dominates world trade today. About half of all world trade in manufactures takes place between the top ten industrial nations: and it is their prosperity which, by and large, determines the prosperity of all the countries bound into the world system of production and distribution.

The manner in which commitment to the international market can strip a country of control over its own affairs has been dramatically illustrated in the past few years by the fortunes of Poland. Until the mid-sixties Polish trade was predominantly with the Soviet bloc, and so the Polish economy was virtually immune to fluctuations in Western economies. Then, in an effort to overcome technological backwardness, the Poles decided to invest heavily in Western machinery, relying on exports of wood, coal, crude minerals and agricultural goods to the booming West to meet the bill. All went reasonably well at first, though domestic inefficiency slowed down the investment programme. But soon this apparently sensible plan was wrecked by the Western crisis of the seventies which followed the oil price rise. The growth of Poland's exports to the West was more than halved, leaving Poland with a huge import bill and massive foreign debts.

The Polish story shows how dangerous it is for peripheral countries to join too wholeheartedly in the world market game. But it is not only the periphery which can suffer. The dependence of national policies on an uncontrolled world system has been the fundamental factor in the crisis of the West. Britain's post-war development has been haunted by the spectre of foreign indebtedness. The relative decline of the United States has been signalled by dollar crises, and the last few years have seen the novel picture of changes in domestic policy being forced on the U.S. government by balance-of-payments problems. The entire international monetary system seems now to be constantly teetering on the edge of crisis, any jolt in the affairs of one country being sufficient to spread disorder among the rest.

As one of the top ten industrial nations, and as a vital financial centre, Britain's past and future are tied to the fortunes of the world system. And the future of that system is entirely dependent upon the establishment of an orderly system for the conduct of trade in manufactures. The financial crises which hit the headlines are primarily a reflection of the disorder which exists in world markets for manufactures. The pound and the dollar are weak because the competitive strength of manufacturing in Britain and in the United States has declined.

In the past decade the world trading system has, of course, suffered a number of major shocks, the most important of which has been the rise in oil prices. But it has been the problems which the manufacturing sector in the United States has suffered over the last fifteen years or so that have rendered the world trading system fundamentally unstable.

The case for free trade

Britain's industrialisation required markets. Free trade was the key. Once potentially troublesome competitors, such as India, had been eliminated, free trade was a device to open up access to markets for the simple basic products that only Britain could mass-produce. However, the economists' case for free trade was presented in somewhat less chauvinistic terms.

Like all economic arguments designed to overwhelm the unconvinced, the British case for free trade was simply that it was in everyone's interest. This was demonstrated by Ricardo.

Comparative advantage

Ricardo argued that each country should produce only those goods in which it had the greatest comparative advantage. The idea was that just as someone who is a mediocre lawyer and an excellent gardener would be better off practising the law and employing someone else to do the garden, so each country would be better off specialising in whatever line it had the greatest relative advantage in and acquiring everything else by trade. Portugal might be able to produce both wine and textiles more cheaply that Britain. But its advantage in wine was so great that, by abandoning production of cloth, concentrating its resources on wine production and charging the British the high price they were willing to pay for wine, it could end up with just as much wine as before and afford to buy more cotton from Britain than it would have produced itself. Portugal should therefore leave industrial production to Britain and join in the benefits of specialisation. Free trade would enforce this desirable outcome.

What is it that determines where comparative advantage lies? Ricardo argued that the different advantages countries possessed in the production of various commodities stemmed from the different levels of technological sophistication they brought to the process of production. Since technology was not constant, but continuously changing, Ricardo's case was incomplete without some account of how technological conditions come to be what they are, and how trade is related to technical progress. This deficiency in his theory was overlooked.

Resource endowments

The modern neo-classical economists support the free-trade argument with a quite different account of the foundations of comparative advantage. They argue that the advantage stems from differences in the resources that countries possess. Countries rich in land, like the United States, should specialise in, and export, land-intensive products; countries with abundant labour, such as India, should export goods which are labour-intensive.

The argument is then extended from natural resources, like land and labour, to modern manufacturing. Advanced industrial countries should export manufactured goods, while Third World countries should be content to specialise in exporting the raw materials and handicrafts in which they have a comparative advantage. So runs the modern free-trade argument.

A flaw in the argument

There is clearly something very wrong with this argument. What was a weakness in Ricardo's story has become a basic error in the neo-classical account. Manufacturing capacity is not a natural resource: it must be built up. And the process of building it up can yield the cumulative benefits of technical change. Trade policy must answer to the principle of cumulative causation.

The weakness of the modern argument for the advantages of free trade was ably exposed in a speech delivered in 1970 by Vice-Minister Y. Ojimi of the Japanese Ministry of International Trade and Industry – MITI, the famous ministry to which so much of Japan's successful economic policy is attributed:

> After the war [said Ojimi] Japan's first exports consisted of such things as toys or other miscellaneous merchandise and low-quality textile products. Should Japan have entrusted its future, according to the theory of comparative advantage, to

these industries characterised by intensive use of labour? That would perhaps be a rational advice for a country with a small population of 5 or 10 million. But Japan has a large population. If the Japanese economy had adopted the simple doctrine of free trade and had chosen to specialise in this kind of industry, it would almost permanently have been unable to break away from the Asian pattern of stagnation and poverty, and would have remained the weakest link in the free world, thereby becoming a problem area in the Far East.

The Ministry of International Trade and Industry decided to establish in Japan industries which require intensive employment of capital and technology, industries that in consideration of comparative cost should be the most inappropriate for Japan, industries such as steel, oil refining, petro-chemicals, automobiles, aircraft, industrial machinery of all sorts, and electronics, including electronic computers. From a short-run, static viewpoint, encouragement of such industries would seem to conflict with economic rationalism. But from a long-range viewpoint, these are precisely the industries where income elasticity of demand is high, technological progress is rapid, and labour productivity rises fast. It was clear that without these industries it would be difficult to employ a population of 100 million and raise their standard of living to that of Europe and America ...'

The Japanese case is an excellent example of the principle of cumulative causation – which we have already used to analyse the rise and fall of industrial regions and countries – now applied to an explanation of international trade. Demand leads to investment and productivity growth, which in turn leads to competitive success, which in turn leads to more demand, and so on. But the crucial link in the chain is *demand*.

The history of the Yamaha company is typical. Founded in the late nineteenth century as instrument makers, Yamaha won a prize for their pianos at the Paris exhibition of 1904. After the Second World War, a sudden explosion of interest in Western music took place in Japan, with a consequent rapid growth of demand for musical instruments. This demand Yamaha supplied. Investment in research led to a crucial breakthrough in light-metal alloys, giving the company a distinct advantage both in wind instruments and in its rapidly expanding motor cycle production. Allied with Japanese skills in electronics, the piano makers could also supply the growing home market for electronic organs. From these home-market platforms they were able to launch an assault on world-markets, in which Yamaha now sells pianos, organs, wind instruments, guitars, tennis rackets, skis and motor cycles.

Cumulative causation

By concentrating production on those commodities for which demand was expected to grow most rapidly, Japan ensured that its manufacturing sector would be locked into the *virtuous* circle of cumulative causation.

It is in the dynamics of the principle of cumulative causation, rather than in the static idea of comparative advantage, that an explanation of the structure and development of trade between the manufacturing countries is to be found. The self-reinforcing dynamic of industrial expansion will ensure that competitive strength is maintained and enhanced. In the longer run, the location of competitive strength may be altered by new institutional arrangements, or by an inability to adapt to the changing market conditions inherent in major inventions, or by the rise of competing nations. But fundamentally the free market works to strengthen the competitive advantage of successful economies and weaken the position of the unsuccessful. The successful will tend increasingly to dominate trade, while the unsuccessful decline.

For it is at the international level that cumulative effects find their most powerful expression. Weakness and strength in manufacturing are mirrored in weakness and strength in the balance-of-payments position.

The balance of payments

The balance-of-payments account lists all the transactions between a country and the rest of the world. Capital transactions cover flows of investment funds, ranging from the purchase and sale of factories to the purchase and sale of stocks and shares and government bonds, which can be bought one day on the money markets of the world and sold the next. Current transactions cover the purchase and sale of goods and services, ranging from raw materials to motor cars to machines to tourism to shipping to financial services.

The final balance of all these transactions is the amount a country owes, or is owed by others. Suppose money is owed by British citizens to citizens of Japan. Japanese exporters are not interested in receiving payment in pounds sterling: their expenses are fixed in yen. So, to pay off the debt, the British importer must acquire yen. For the country as a whole, this will mean either drawing on national reserves of yen or, more usually, borrowing yen, either from the exporting country – say, from a Japanese bank, or the Japanese government – or from a third party – say, a German bank with reserves of yen to lend.

If the balance of payments fluctuates from year to year around a balance of zero, periods of borrowing will tend to balance out periods of lending. Reserves of yen can be replenished and loans repaid.

Trade in the modern world is a complicated business, and the yen may be earned by multi-lateral trade. For example, Britain may have a deficit with Japan but acquire the necessary yen by running a surplus with Australia, which in turn sells iron ore to Japan, thus earning the yen the British need, and so on. But despite these complications, all that really matters is that the balance of payments with the rest of the world as a whole should roughly balance. The system will then be reasonably stable.

A persistent deficit

But if there is a systematic tendency for a country to be in deficit – to be a borrower from the rest of the world – something has to be done. Reserves will eventually run out, and debt cannot be accumulated indefinitely. Ultimately, creditors will not be willing to lend any more to a delinquent borrower, and the borrowing country will not be able to buy more on international markets than it can pay for directly with its exports. It will be forced to cut imports, both by limiting the purchases of foreign goods by consumers and by slowing down the output of import-using industries – perhaps precipitating a major cut in living standards. Since this dire outcome must be avoided, the need to preserve, on average, balanced international payments is a fundamental constraint on any government's freedom of manoeuvre in economic affairs.

A persistent deficit must be eliminated. But how is this to be done?

On the capital account action may be taken to restrict outflow and encourage investment from abroad. A considerable part of the outflow of capital may be devoted to the purchase of foreign government bonds or foreign stocks and shares. This will yield some useful revenue in the future but has no direct relevance to the development of the domestic economy and could therefore be dispensed with. Encouraging foreign investment in home bonds or stocks and shares is not easy for a deficit country and, anyhow, less attractive as an option. Investment of this type may require high interest rates to satisfy a foreign lender, and the money can rapidly flow out again on the whim of foreign investors, perhaps precipitating a financial crisis.

What to do about investment in productive assets is more problematic. Some foreign investment is directly connected with trade – setting up dealers abroad, for example – and cutting this investment may harm exports. Investment in production facilities abroad may well harm the home economy, but may be seen as necessary to maintain the competitiveness of British companies. Foreign investment in Britain may both be a welcome boost to the balance of payments and bring with it technological and managerial benefits; but it means that a larger proportion of domestic industry will be foreign-owned and, in consequence, less readily amenable to government policies formulated in the national interest.

All in all, much can be done to cut a wasteful outflow of investment funds. The criterion to be applied is whether the flow of funds aids or inhibits the maintenance of a high rate of growth of demand for the products of domestic manufacturing. None the less it is ultimately the current account that matters. A one-way flow of borrowing cannot continue indefinitely. Some way must be found for a deficit country to cut imports and increase exports.

Devaluation

The orthodox solution is devaluation – that is, reducing the exchange rate between the home currency and the currencies of competitors. The British devaluation of 1967, for example, reduced the rate of exchange of the pound against the dollar from $2.80 to the pound to $2.40. The objective of a devaluation is to make home-country exports cheaper abroad; imports from abroad will be more expensive and hence discouraged. Changes in the exchange rate may take place at discrete intervals, as they did in the fifties and sixties, or they may vary from day to day according to the relative supplies of, and demand for, currencies on money markets around the world, as was the case in the seventies.

If variation in the exchange rate has the desired effect on imports and exports, it may be used as an automatic mechanism to keep the balance of payments in balance. Flows of imports and exports are reflected in supplies of, and demands for, a currency on the foreign exchange markets of the world. The automatic workings of these markets can be used to alter the relative value of currencies and so solve balance-of-payments problems.

Unfortunately things don't work quite so smoothly.

The increase in import prices that follows a fall in the exchange rate means that many workers face increased bills for food and household goods and companies face higher costs of production due to the increased costs of imported materials or machines. So, to maintain their profits, companies push up prices. Soon all the competitive advantage gained by the devaluation has been wiped out by the acceleration in inflation, and another devaluation is required. This leads to yet more inflation, another devaluation and so on, in a rapidly increasing spiral.

Many countries have been caught in this devaluation-inflation trap in the last few years – including Israel, where the schekel was devalued by 600 per cent against the dollar between 1974 and 1979 and inflation is now well over 100 per cent per year, and Argentina, where the peso was devalued over the same period from 4 pesos to the dollar to 1,500 and inflation has been as high as 500 per cent per year.

The only way to limit the inflationary consequences of a devaluation is by forcing workers to take cuts in their living standards by not responding to higher prices with increased wage demands. It is not by chance that devaluations tend to be accompanied by incomes policies, the role of which has been precisely to limit the inflationary impact of the devaluation and to cut spending on imports by reducing real wages.

The effects of a devaluation are further reduced by the fact that competition in manufactures is not merely a matter of price. Throughout the fifties and sixties and in the early seventies, British goods were relatively cheap on world markets, but consumers have none the less preferred German, French and Japanese cars, French and Italian household goods and Japanese televisions. And producers *must* buy the best German machines if they are to stay competitive. The important role of non-price factors in determining the competitiveness of manufactures significantly reduces the impact of a devaluation. So small devaluations are not going to work. And the large devaluation necessary to make some impact is not going to work either, for it will set off an inflationary spiral that will rapidly nullify any beneficial effects.

The automatic mechanism of devaluation is therefore unlikely to be a solution. It certainly has not solved Britain's persistent balance-of-payments problems. This is not to say that when prices are a long way out of line some adjustment of the exchange rate may not be necessary. Exchange rates are not immutably fixed. A country's goods can be excessively expensive as well as uncompetitive in non-price terms, and in this case devaluation may be part of a package designed to solve the problem. But it will be the measures taken to break out of a negative circle of cumulative causation that really matter. Devaluation can only play a supporting role.

On the other hand, a country that is competitive in non-price terms may use devaluation as a device to increase its already healthy market share. Italy has pursued this strategy over the last twenty-five years.

Deflation

If devaluation will not solve a chronic deficit, what 'more decisive' policies are available? The only other market solution is deflation. This involves the government in deliberately setting out to lower economic activity at home, deliberately creating unemployment, so that workers can no longer afford to buy imports and manufacturers with falling sales no longer need imported inputs. This solution will work. If a government is willing to make its own citizens poor enough – say, by making enough of them unemployed – imports will be cut; and if exports hold up, the balance of payments will be brought back into balance.

But it will be a pyrrhic victory. The improvement in the balance of payments has been achieved by slowing down the growth rate in demand. This sets the principle of cumulative causation working in reverse. Cuts in investment and productivity growth weaken the long-run competitive position of the economy. So deflation solves the temporary problem, but it makes the underlying problems worse.

This is exactly the story of Britain since the war. The notorious stops in the stop-go cycle succeeded in their immediate purpose of improving the balance of payments position. They also ensured that each crisis was worse than the one which preceded it. The rate of growth of demand was slow and frequently interrupted. Productivity growth was correspondingly slow. Britain slipped further behind.

Deflation on a world scale

So neither of the market solutions, devaluation and deflation, will solve the problem of a country in Britain's position, in which the manufacturing sector is increasingly uncompetitive. It is in the international context that the awesome power of the principle of cumulative causation is starkly revealed. The strong countries will tend to be in balance-of-payments surplus and so will be able to expand steadily without fear of an insupportable increase in imports, and this expansion will, by stimulating productivity growth, fuel their competitive strength. The weak, on the other hand, will be in perpetual deficit, forced to devalue and deflate, reinforcing their competitive weakness.

Indeed the story has a yet more cruel twist in its tail.

By definition, everything that is imported by someone must have been exported by someone; so the total value of world exports is exactly equal to – indeed, is one and the same thing as – the total value of the world's imports. The values of imports and exports are not, of course, equal for each country; but since the totals are the same, the surplus or deficit of all the individual countries must collectively add up to zero. If one country runs a surplus, someone, somewhere, must have a deficit.

Suppose the deficit countries deflate hard in a successful attempt to get rid of their deficit. Since the deficits have gone, the surpluses will have gone too. When the previously surplus countries find that their surpluses have disappeared, they will tend to deflate or devalue a little in an attempt to recover their former strength. If they are successful, the old deficit countries will find their deficits reappearing and they will be forced to deflate yet further, causing the surplus countries to deflate again – and so on and so on. The entire international system has a built-in deflationary bias. It will always tend to push the world into depression.

The origins of this automatic tendency towards depression lie in the inability of the market system to manage international trading relations in an orderly manner.

The role of the Big Spender

But just a moment! Hasn't this world system worked in the past? What about the 'Golden Age' of the West after the Second World War, when trade barriers were dismantled and international trade and world production grew faster than ever before? Indeed, what about the whole history of the nineteenth century that created the modern world? The system has worked before. How can it now be indicated as a cause of Britain's troubles?

The clue to the answers to these questions may be found in the simple point that one country's deficit is another country's surplus. Suppose there is one country that can afford to run a permanent deficit. This country may have a surplus of exports over imports but invests or lends an amount at least as great as that surplus. If this Big Spender does run a deficit overall, the rest of the world can enjoy a surplus. The deflationary bias of the system will be overcome and world-wide expansion is possible.

To do the trick, the Big Spender must not only be willing and able to spend but must also have some power to organise trade and oversee financial affairs. Otherwise some chronic-deficit countries may drag the system down, or financial crises may disrupt the expansion drive. A combination of economic and political power is required. This combination was found in Britain in the nineteenth century, and in the post-Second World War era in the United States.

Britain as Big Spender

Nineteenth-century Britain was the manufacturing and financial centre of the world. The fabled Gold Standard mechanism of those years was, in fact, not an automatic mechanism but a system manipulated from London. This is not to pretend that there lurked in the London money markets an unseen planning board. It is rather that London worked according to an established set of rules – rules which included the support of deficit countries by loans to their governments and which were framed with the overall objective of promoting trade. It is true that the system looked a good deal more harmonious seen from London than it did from countries on the periphery, but this did not matter too much in terms of the system as a whole as long as London was prepared to finance overall expansion. And this it was prepared to do. Indeed the system proved so successful that in the latter half of the nineteenth century, when Britain's dominance of world markets for manufactures was slipping away, British economic strength was maintained by the flow of profits from earlier loans and investments – profits which were then re-lent to finance the further expansion of world trade.

The United States as Big Spender

The United States played a similar role after the Second World War, though now the actors were more self-aware and the plot was better understood. The economic dominance of the United States at the end of the war could have threatened the stability of the world trading system. Everyone wanted American goods, and the United States ran a massive surplus of exports over imports. European deficits could not have been sustained, and European reconstruction would have been impossible, without a massive outflow of American funds in investments, loans and Marshall Aid. Instead of a mythical Gold Standard (it had really been a Sterling Standard from the word go), the world was now on a Dollar Standard, and it was the United States which, either directly or through international agencies, managed the international trading system.

Demise of the Big Spender

But when no Big Spender is available the deflationary bias of the world market system takes over. In the inter-war period the British role of world banker could no longer be sustained. The idea that financial manipulation by the Bank of England was sufficient to maintain order on world markets had been a myth all along. It had been the world economic (and political) dominance of Britain that mattered. Now no amount of fiddling by the Bank would do.

While Britain was unable, the United States was unwilling to play the role of world banker. In spite of being thrust into the centre of world economic affairs after the First World War, United States' policy was still fundamentally inward-looking – as exemplified by the persistent tendency to cut imports and foreign lending *at the same time*, a sure recipe for international instability and the reverse of the behaviour of nineteenth-century Britain.

The post-Second World War United States has been conscious of its role as economic leader of the Western world. But its leadership has been undermined by the relative decline of American manufacturing industry and the consequent deterioration of the United States' balance of payments. The fundamental change in the balance-of-payments account has been the steady deterioration in trade in manufactures, particularly manufactured consumer goods. Throughout the fifties trade in consumer goods showed a positive balance, but through the sixties and seventies it became more and more negative, until in the early seventies the negative balance on consumer goods outweighed the positive balance on machines and other investment goods. The United States had become a net importer of manufactures. Its economic strength was now to be maintained by earnings from foreign investments and exports of raw materials, especially foodstuffs. The largest industrial economy in the world maintains its balance of payments by non-industrial means.

The decline in the relative economic strength of the United States knocked the dollar from its pedestal and robbed the United States government of its ability to sustain the expansion of the world economy by greater lending. Some semblance of order has been maintained by the continued political dominance of the United States in the West. The international economic bickering of the inter-war years has been prevented, or at least limited, by the position of the United States as defender of last resort. In effect, the coherence and stability of the West depends on the existence of the Soviet Union.

None the less the world system is no longer managed from Washington or New York; and despite the considerably greater understanding of economic affairs which modern governments possess vis-à-vis their inter-war counterparts, the world system has re-asserted its deflationary power. The international trading and financial system has begun to acquire the characteristic instability of the 1930s.

So the international free market system works relatively smoothly when it is organised by one dominant power – that is, when it is not simply a free market system!

Even then the market conspires against a harmonious solution, for ultimately the role of the Big Spender is difficult to sustain. Not only does the perpetual deficit maintained by the Big Spender mean that other countries must absorb more and more of its currency: the Big

Spender is also boosting demand in other economies, and its relative position will in due course tend to decline. So the Americans bought up a large amount of Europe after the war with cheques the Europeans never cashed – they just added the dollars to their reserves. But, paradoxically, this was ultimately to the benefit of the fast-growing European economies and to the detriment of the economy of the United States.

An international solution?

If no nation can play the role of perpetual Big Spender in an unstable world market system, why cannot there be some sort of international organisation which disciplines the international market?

It was in the attempt to establish just such an international system that the Allies met at Bretton Woods in July 1944. The chaos of the 1930s was fresh in the memory, and a new system of international organisation was sought by all.

Keynes was the leader of the British delegation. In the 1930s he had argued that the only solution to the disruption spread by international markets was for countries to turn inwards, to cut themselves off, as far as was possible from international trading relations:

> We do not wish [Keynes had argued in 1933] to be at the mercy of world forces working out, or trying to work out some uniform equilibrium according to the ideal principles, if they can be called such, of *laissez-faire* capitalism ... It is my central contention ... that we all need to be as free as possible from economic changes elsewhere, in order to make our own favourite experiments ... and that a deliberate movement towards greater national self-sufficiency will make our own task easier ... Ideas, knowledge, science, hospitality, travel – these are things which should of their nature be international. But let goods be homespun whenever it is reasonable and conveniently possible, and above all, let finance be primarily national ...

But by the late thirties, Keynes had changed his mind. His new ideas on how to manage the national economy could, he believed, be extended to management of the international economy. He proposed the establishment of an international central bank which would manage the overall level and composition of world demand by lending to deficit countries, and by penalising surplus countries with an interest charge on their surpluses.

Keynes's conversion to an international solution sat well with the dominant strain in American thinking, which regarded the enthusiasm for national solutions as both economically and politically dangerous. As Dean Acheson, then a leading administrator in the State Department, put it in 1944:

> We cannot go through another ten years like the ten years at the end of the Twenties and the beginning of the Thirties, without having the most far-reaching consequences upon our economic and social system ... when we look at that problem we may say that it is a problem of markets. You don't have a problem of production. The United States has unlimited creative energy. The important thing is markets. We have got to see that what the country produces is used and is sold under financial arrangements which make its production possible ... You must look to foreign markets. If you wish to control the entire trade and income of the United States, which means the life of the people, you could probably fix it so that everything produced here would be consumed here, but that would completely change our constitution, our relations to property, human liberty, our very conceptions of law. And nobody contemplates that. Therefore, you find you must look to other markets and those markets are abroad ...

The Americans did not, despite their agreement with Keynes's general perspective, accept his idea of a powerful supra-national agency. The nation that was undisputed top-dog was not going to be told how to manage its affairs by a group of international bureaucrats. So, instead of an international central bank, we got the IMF, the International Monetary Fund. The IMF was to have powers to lend to deficit countries, but it had no *effective* power to penalise surplus countries and so manage the structure of world demand. (There was a provision known as the 'scarce currency' clause which allowed discrimination against a country whose currency was declared 'scarce' because it ran a persistent surplus.

But the only scarce currency immediately after the war was the dollar, and not only was the U.S. running the system but also everyone desperately wanted American goods, so the clause was never invoked.)

While the United States maintained the stability of demand in the world system, the IMF could play a subsidiary role in maintaining the Dollar Standard by aiding deficit countries. But with the decline of the United States, the IMF has become an agency of financial discipline, enforcing strict deflationary policies on any deficit country desperate enough to wish to borrow. The IMF has completely failed to provide any expansionary leadership, and has become a byword for deflation.

But it must be admitted that the whole concept of an international agency as Big Spender is untenable, and that even Keynes's plan suffered from a fundamental flaw. The Big Spender must be economically dominant and must have the political power to enforce unpopular decisions. An international agency cannot possibly, at least in the current scheme of things, have such power; and so it cannot possibly fulfill the managerial role that is required.

Other sources of instability today

I have argued that the structure of world trade in manufactures, with the tendency for international institutional arrangements to reinforce the cumulative tendencies of competition in manufactures, is the basic element in the instability of the world system today. But this instability is exacerbated by three other factors.

First, and certainly most visible, is the rapid rise in oil prices which has taken place since 1973. The oil price rise has led to the accumulation of massive balance-of-payments surpluses in many, though not all, OPEC countries. Try as they might, it is very difficult for some of the oil exporters, particularly the Gulf states, to spend all their income. Their surpluses are mirrored in the deficits of the industrial countries and of Third World countries.

The immediate reaction of the Western countries to the deficits created by the increased price of oil was to deflate hard, cutting their imports from each other and from Third World suppliers of raw materials. The short-term result of this was to shift the deficit on to the weaker industrial countries and on to the Third World (and the unfortunate Poland). The long-term result has been a protracted recession, from which the Western system has been, as yet, unable to escape.

Has OPEC created the recession? Only in the sense that it provided the push which knocked over the unstable system. The rise in the price of oil meant that some of the goods and services produced in the West which had previously been consumed at home would be transferred to oil-producing states. This constitutes a loss of income to Western citizens. But the loss of income due to the deflationary policies followed by Western governments was, in the period 1973-1980, four times greater than the loss due to the higher oil price. It is the inability of the system to absorb shocks without turning on itself and consuming its own children that is the real basis of the world recession.

If it were possible to organise the West in an expansionary drive on the scale of the sixties, it is probable that the drive would be cut short by a shortage of energy reserves and by a new explosion of oil prices. Energy policies designed to reduce dependence on oil should, therefore, be an important component of a general recovery. Given time, technological progress can reduce the demand for oil. But time will not lead to a new method of organising international trade. Without a new method, reduced dependence on oil will not solve the problems of the Western system.

A second factor which has contributed to instability is the increasing sophistication and flexibility of the world financial system, which has greatly enhanced the ability of firms, banks and individuals to move money around the world looking for the safest and most remunerative haven. This process results in massive flows of money from one country to another, creating chaos in the foreign exchanges and forcing on governments economic policy measures which are quite irrelevant to the underlying problems of their economies. The very high level of the foreign exchange rate of the pound in 1980, which created considerable difficulties for exporters of manufactures, was due to just such speculative flows – aided and abetted, it must be said, by government interest-rate policy.

A third destabilising factor, which derives from the same sophistication of the banking mechanism, is the weakening of control of national governments over their own financial systems. Countries with rather free-and-easy banking laws, such as the UK, have permitted the establishment of expatriate banking funds in their territory. The most famous of these is the so-called Euro-dollar market in the City of London. Dollars held in London banks are lent with less than the degree of care that would be enforced in the United States, creating a potentially serious weakness at the core of the world financial system. Euro-dollar loans to sustain the faltering Brazilian economy have reached such proportions that Brazil may default. This would ruin some major American banks and plunge the Western financial system into chaos.

These three factors contribute to the troubles of the disorderly and unmanaged world trading system. And there is no sign of any new manager appearing in the next decade or so. Indeed the vestigial managerial powers of the United States are likely to decline still further as its relative economic decline continues apace. The international trading system is less able to weather occasional squalls than it was twenty years ago. But too often it is the squalls that are blamed, rather than the leaky boat.

A peculiarity of current economic debate is that the problems of world trade are not high on the agenda. That agenda is topped by inflation.

6

Inflation: Symptom or Disease?

The acceleration in the rate of inflation during the last decade has made it a central issue in economic policy. But is it really a Bad Thing? And is it a cause or a consequence of other economic problems? Theories of inflation can be categorised in terms of the fundamental divide among economists: those that portray the market as an automatically functioning mechanism, and those that reject this view. Keynes's analysis of inflation focussed both on the role of demand and on the role of costs. The inflation of the seventies discredited simple demand-side unemployment-inflation trade-offs. The monetarists made a comeback arguing that growth of the money supply causes inflation. They stress the automatic role of the market, but have difficulty explaining how the quantity of money is to be controlled. The 'institutional' view of inflation argues that inflation is the consequence of failure of the market to maintain full employment and growth.

* * *

In a society in which economic life is organised by flows of money, and in which economic power and even personal survival are determined by the ownership of money, inflation is inevitably a nuisance, and perhaps a danger. For inflation means a continuous rise in money prices and money incomes, so that money is, quite literally, worth less and less as time goes by.

Prices today are higher than they have ever been before. Comparisons are, of course, difficult. A television set in 1980 is quite different from a television set in 1950, and so comparing their prices is not really an accurate estimate of the real change in the value of money. The same is true of almost all manufactured goods. But there are *some* eternal verities. A pint of best bitter cost the – to me – staggering sum of thirteen shillings in January 1982, an amount that somehow sounds far greater than 65 new pence. Thirty years before that same pint would have cost only one shilling. Even a decade ago, it cost only two shillings and fourpence (or, if you like, $11\frac{1}{2}$ new pence).

Comparable increases have occurred in the price of bread, a loaf costing only $2\frac{1}{4}$ new pence in 1950, 9 pence in 1970, and 36 pence in 1980. Similarly, a gallon of four-star petrol cost only 15 new pence in 1950, 32 new pence in 1970, and 127 new pence in 1980.

These increases have been matched – indeed, in many years more than matched – by increases in incomes. The average weekly earnings of adult male workers in manufacturing were £7.67 in 1950, £28.05 in 1970 and £113.06 in 1980. So, despite price increases, people are much better off today than they were thirty years ago.

None the less we are told that the continuous rise in money prices and money incomes since the war has ruined Britain's competitiveness, has eroded the incentive to invest, has created unemployment and is even threatening the fabric of democracy. Inflation is a Bad Thing.

It has always been a Bad Thing, but the acceleration of the rate of inflation in the last ten years has forced the issue into the centre of economic policy debate. Instead of inflation being seen as a nuisance which might be the price to be paid for achieving other objectives – full employment, for example – now, reducing the rate of inflation has become *the* objective, the substance and the symbol of a successful economic policy.

Is this wise? Is inflation the *cause* of our problems, or the *consequence*?

The answer to this central question depends on what the cause of inflation itself is believed to be, and on an assessment of whether any prescribed cure is worse than the disease.

At first sight inflation appears to be a totally irrational phenomenon. Doubling all wages and doubling all prices would leave very nearly everyone back where they started. So what is the point of the whole exercise? Does inflation have a role to play in the operations of the market mechanism? Or is it an aberration, imposed on the market by the foolish policies of governments, or by the self-defeating greed of trade unions or corporations?

Inflation and theories of the market system

There are almost as many views of what causes inflation as there are economists. But *we* can make sense of the cacophony. For basically all the different views boil down to those two different interpretations of how the market works which we have already seen produce the fundamental divide in economic thinking. On the one hand are those who believe that in spite of temporary hiccups and short-run deviations the market will, if uninhibited by institutional constraints, ensure that the economy operates at a full-employment level of activity. On the other are those who believe that no such automatic mechanism exists – that markets just don't work that way.

It is the first group – those who have faith in the market mechanism – who have made the running in economic affairs over the past ten years or so, for this group contains, indeed is dominated by, the monetarists.

Keynes's analysis of inflation

Before the monetarist takeover, thinking on inflation was dominated by ideas which were more in tune with the second position, being founded on no particular conception of an automatically functioning market. Most of these ideas were derived in one way or another from Keynes's remarkable pamphlet *How to Pay for the War*, published in 1940.

At the outbreak of the war Keynes was concerned that the wartime operation of the economy should not spark off a rapid inflation. This, in itself, would be bad for morale, and could lead to social conflict and accusations of profiteering. The experience of the First World War had not been propitious.

Keynes identified two separate, though related, factors contributing to inflation.

First, the very high pressure of demand associated with wartime production would result in prices being continually bid up. Consumer goods, materials and labour would all be in short supply. Therefore rising consumer goods prices would not choke off demand, for wages would be bid up too, maintaining their buying power and keeping up the pressure of demand. The price level could explode.

Secondly, the rise in prices would in itself lead to pressure to increase money-wages as workers attempted to prevent the erosion of living standards. The very notion of 'the cost of living' implies that wage-earners have a clear conception of what they expect to be able to buy with their wages.

Keynes proposed a two-part programme to attack the two sides of the inflationary process. To cut demand, he argued that, as well as reducing take-home pay by increased taxation, spending should be cut by compulsory saving – the famous post-war credits. This would have the dual advantage both of being less painful than taxation and of storing up purchasing power to maintain demand after the war. In fact, unlike the First, the Second World War was not followed by a slump, and repayment of post-war credits was delayed to avoid increasing demand in an already buoyant economy, so bringing an eminently clever scheme into some disrepute.

To take the pressure off working-class wage-packets, Keynes proposed the stabilisation of the prices of necessities by appropriate subsidies. In the event subsidies had to be combined with rationing to cope with the severe shortages of many basic foodstuffs and other consumer goods. But it is a striking fact that during the war standards of nutrition and living standards in general rose – the result of careful planning and full employment.

The unemployment-inflation trade-off

It was the demand side of Keynes's analysis that was to dominate post-war thinking on inflation. The idea that inflation is caused by the pressure of overall demand was formalised into a trade-off between unemployment and inflation known as the Phillips Curve (after A.W. Phillips, whose 1958 article launched the curve as a formal, empirical relationship). Higher unemployment means lower inflation. Lower unemployment means higher inflation. When demand was high and unemployment low, it was argued, trade unions would be able to bid up money wages and employers would be willing to pay, for they could easily raise prices on the buoyant market. When unemployment was high, however, wages and prices would rise more slowly.

The idea of a trade-off was portrayed by some writers in such mechanical terms that it became for them a fact of economic life, rather as the action of a lever is a fact of mechanics. There was believed to be a given fixed relationship between inflation and unemployment. It could be confidently argued, therefore, that if unemployment were to rise to a specified level inflation would cease altogether. The level was set at about 650,000 unemployed.

The idea of a simple trade-off between inflation and unemployment was totally discredited in the 1970s when unemployment and inflation rose simultaneously – and both went on rising at an accelerating pace. Numerous attempts were made to save the Phillips Curve by offering explanations as to why the curve had shifted. But it was soon clear that what was happening was all shift and no curve. The simple demand-determined theory of inflation was doomed.

In the resulting confusion monetarism, the main pre-Keynesian theory of inflation, made a triumphant comeback.

The foundations of monetarism

The monetarist case begins from the proposition that the amount of money that changes hands, say, in a year, must be equal to the value of all transactions in that year.

The amount of money that changes hands is equal to the quantity of money in circulation multiplied by the number of times it is used in a year. A given pound note, for example, might be used in many transactions during the year. (It is a matter of great dispute whether the number of times the stock of money is used, the so-called velocity of circulation, may reasonably be taken as fixed. Whether it may or not affects the extent to which there is a simple relationship between the quantity of money and the price level. The monetarists argue that velocity is stable. But since there are far more fundamental issues to debate, this aspect of the monetarist controversy will be ignored in what follows.)

The value of transactions in a year is equal to the number of goods and services produced and sold multiplied by the average price level.

The proposition relating the amount of money to the value of output is a truism. But like so many truisms it can be invested with great analytical power. Suppose the number of times money is used in the year is fixed. Then, if the quantity of money is increased *and* the number of transactions is unchanged, the average price level must also increase. Equally, if the price level is higher, the quantity of money must be higher too.

But what is cause and what is effect? The debate about whether the cause was higher prices or a greater money supply raged throughout the nineteenth century, and the same arguments are being reproduced today. The monetarist position, of course, is that a faster growth of the money supply causes a higher rate of inflation.

Monetarists come in all shapes and sizes, and their ideas are often presented at quite extraordinary levels of abstruse mathematical and/or statistical argument. But the basic principles underlying all monetarist thinking, and all monetarist policy measures, are quite simple.

The first, and most important, principle is that the quantity of output and the level of employment is *given*, apart from the occasional temporary fluctuation.

The second, which follows directly from the first, is that if the supply of money in the economy is increased, then, since more money is chasing the same quantity of output, prices must rise.

So, to understand what monetarism is all about, we need to answer two questions: What determines the supply of money, and what determines the quantity of output?

The quantity of money

Let us begin with the quantity of money. What is money? It is clearly not only the cash in your pocket. It is also the current account at the bank on which you can issue cheques. It is the credit card with which you can buy the things you have always wanted but cannot afford. It is anything which is generally acceptable in payment of a debt. So, in the confusion of post-war Germany, when cigarettes and nylon stockings were the generally accepted instruments of commerce, cigarettes and nylon stockings *were* money.

As *anything* which is generally acceptable can be money, how can we make any sense of the notion of a money supply which the government can control?

Since gold coins ceased to circulate money has consisted of tokens which are backed only by the government – by political power, if you like. The 'promise to pay' one pound printed on every pound note really amounts to a government commitment to ensure that you can buy one pound's worth of goods with that piece of paper – in other words, to ensure that that piece of paper is generally acceptable. If the system of government collapsed, the monetary system would collapse with it. To keep daily life going, people would then use things which have value in themselves, such as cigarettes, as money.

The government prints the banknotes. Its decisions about printing are therefore an important component in the determination of the money supply. But cash is only a small proportion of what is generally acceptable as money. The largest component of the money stock is our current-account balances at the bank, supplemented by deposit and savings accounts, accounts at building societies and a wide variety of other assets which can be turned into spending power at will. How does the government control these?

The answer lies in the relationship between government financial transactions and the operation of the banking system as a whole. Since the authority of the state is the ultimate backing of the value of money, the system runs on what the government prints and issues. The government does not simply print pound notes. It also prints and issues a wide variety of paper assets by means of which it borrows from the public to finance the day-to-day running of the state and, perhaps, longer-term deficits too. Some borrowings are very short term, the government paying up in three months or so. Some are very long. Some indeed are irredeemable, the government promising to pay a fixed return for ever, but never repaying the capital sum. The typical short-term borrowing is made by means of three-month Treasury Bills. Longer-term bonds, the so-called gilt-edged stock, culminate in irredeemable Consols (short for consolidated stock). The short-term character of Treasury Bills means that they are readily marketable at or near their face value. Gilt-edged stock, however, can fluctuate widely in value depending on supplies and demands in the bond market.

The banking system is composed of a wide variety of financial institutions, but it is dominated by the major clearing banks, the branches of which line High Streets – and not so high streets – throughout the country. The role of the major banks is to accept deposits from the public – primarily in the form of current accounts and savings accounts – and to lend them out to the public as personal loans, overdrafts and advances to companies.

Long experience has taught the banks that they need keep only a relatively small proportion of their deposits in cash, or in their own current account with the Bank of England, or in so-called liquid assets, such as Treasury Bills or money lent to other financial institutions that may be recalled at a moment's notice. The rest may be lent on a longer-term basis. The banks are able to do this because holders of deposits seldom ask for their money back in cash. They are content to treat their deposits as money, they have no need for cash. Suppose, for example, that the bank advances you an overdraft. You write a cheque to pay a bill, and the shopkeeper deposits that cheque into the banking system. There is no demand on the system for cash.

Prudence requires that some cash and other liquid assets are held to cover the day-to-day demands on the banking system for cash and the needs of settling accounts between the banks themselves. Prudence is reinforced by statutory requirements laid down by the Bank of England. A major duty of the Bank of England is to maintain a stable financial system. If a bank kept too little cash or other liquid assets on hand, it might be caught short by a temporary increase in the demand for cash from its customers, be forced to close its doors and precipitate a loss of confidence in the entire banking community. So the Bank of England lays down strict rules as to proportions to be maintained between the banks' liquid assets and other assets, such as loans to the public and long-dated government stock.

Control of the money supply

Here is a relationship between government financial transactions and the expansion of the main component of the money supply, bank deposits. Since the government controls the quantity of cash and Treasury Bills in circulation, it can affect the quantity of liquid assets available to the banking system as a whole. As the maximum level of bank lending is a fixed multiple of the quantity of liquid assets, the government, by varying this quantity or by changing the rules of the game – forcing the banks to hold a larger proportion of liquid assets, for example – can enforce a cut in lending.

Suppose the government regards the level of bank lending as too high. It can then sell some gilt-edged stock, so withdrawing cash from the economy, or it can cut back on Treasury Bill sales, or both. The value of gilt-edged stock fluctuates too much for the banks to be able to treat it as a reliable reserve. The total amount of liquid reserves will therefore have fallen, and the banks will either have to cut back on advances or raise interest rates to persuade the public to deposit more cash. The trouble is that, to persuade people to buy the long-dated bonds, the government may well have to pay them a higher rate of interest too. So interest rates will have a general tendency to rise. Control of the money supply and control of interest rates are incompatible policies. If you have a target for the money supply, you must be prepared to let interest rates be what they will. And if you have a target for interest rates – say, to keep down the cost of mortgages or the cost of borrowing to industry – you must be prepared to let the money supply be what it will.

Manipulating the money supply by buying and selling different sorts of bills and bonds may be more difficult than usual if the government is running an overall deficit. The fact that government spending is greater than income from taxation means that the government is forced to borrow, or to print the money. If it hopes to avoid increasing the quantity of liquid assets in circulation, the government must borrow by selling gilt-edged stock, long bonds. Increases in government spending will tend to raise income and saving, and so facilitate sale of gilts. But for any given level of spending more gilts can normally be sold only by offering a higher rate of interest, forcing up rates throughout the money market and eliciting cries of anguish from mortgage holders and industry. This is one of the reasons why the monetarists are opposed to government deficits, and are so keen on cutting government spending.

But even if the government does, at the cost of high interest rates, control the amount of cash and Treasury Bills in circulation, can it really control the supply of money? All evidence shows that within reasonable bounds it cannot. The problem is that the financial system of a country like Britain is too flexible and sophisticated to be easily controlled. As soon as the government specifies some set of monetary assets the issue of which will be strictly controlled, the financial system finds ways of being less dependent on those assets than it was before, and carries on regardless.

The corset

The finest example of the ability of a modern financial system to evade government control is to be found in the history of the corset. The 'corset' is the term applied to direct restrictions placed by the Bank of England on lending by banks and other financial institutions. In 1979, worried by the rate of expansion of the money supply, the government instructed the Bank of England to tighten restrictions on a wide category of lending activities by the commercial banks. It worked. The growth of lending slowed down, and the growth of the money supply as *conventionally* measured slowed down too. Like all corsets, however, what was squeezed in one place popped out in another. A form of money known as 'trade acceptances' was used by large companies to overcome the shortage of bank loans. These were basically IOUs, which companies could use to obtain credit if a financial institution, such as a bank, were willing to *accept* the IOU – that is, to guarantee its value. This, for a suitable fee, the banks were willing to do. Trade acceptances were not part of the money supply as conventionally measured. So, although they were being used as a means of expanding credit, the 'money supply' did not grow. When the corset was taken off in June 1980 the money supply exploded, as companies switched from what had been a rather expensive way of obtaining credit back to conventional overdrafts and loans.

This experience, and many others like it, suggests that the quantity of money in the economy is determined not by the supply but by the demand. If someone is willing to pay enough, the financial community can supply the credit one way or another.

The level of output

But what of the other pillar of the monetarist argument – the related propositions that the level of output and employment will be determined by the real forces of supply and demand, that these levels may be treated as given from the point of view of monetary policy, and that these levels will be associated with full employment?

Actually the argument as to which level of employment will be determined by the market is a little more refined. The monetarists argue that any inhibition to the operations of the market – the behaviour of trade unions, for example, or the provision of welfare benefits to the unemployed – will mean that the level of employment achieved may not be at a conventionally defined level of full employment. None the less, in so far as these inhibitions are part and parcel of the economic system at any given time, the level of employment determined by the market is the 'natural level' to which the economy will always gravitate. As Milton Friedman, guru of the monetarists, has put it, the natural level of unemployment 'is the level that would be found out by the equations of supply and demand provided there is embedded in them the actual structural characteristics of the labour and commodity markets, including market imperfections ...' The fewer the imperfections limiting the operations of the free market, the more nearly will the natural level of unemployment correspond to full employment. But, at whatever level, the market determines the 'natural' rate – and how can what is 'natural' be so bad?

Here we have the truly fundamental principle of monetarism, the touchstone of the true monetarist economist. The normal operations of the economy are such as to ensure that, on average, the economy operates at full employment of people and machines. If institutional arrangements interfere in the free workings of the market, there may be unemployment. But if the market can be left to operate freely, even this unemployment will be kept to a minimum as the economy gravitates to its natural level of operation. So the best government policies are those which interfere least in the workings of the market, other than by aiding its operation – by weakening trade unions and cutting unemployment benefits, for example, or by cutting government spending, which only creates inflation or pushes up interest rates and which also reduces the resources available to the market.

The critics

Since the belief in the automatic functioning of the market is central to the entire monetarist programme, if this proposition is false the entire programme is built on false premises.

This is exactly what the opponents of monetarism argue. Although a somewhat diverse group, focussing their criticisms on different aspects of the monetarist edifice, they basically follow Keynes in arguing that the market does not automatically ensure full employment, or even the attainment of a 'natural rate' of unemployment. This part of the monetarist argument is quite simply wrong.

But dismissing monetarism is not enough. After the confusion of the early seventies, what do the opponents have to offer as a positive alternative?

An alternative theory

Here the picture is less clear, with a variety of ideas on inflation being developed or simply resuscitated. But a leading strand in alternative thinking on the nature and causes of inflation has been constructed from those elements of Keynes's wartime analysis which were neglected in the early mechanical inflation-unemployment trade-off theories. Inflation is now to be explained in terms of the institutional structure of a modern market economy – in terms of the behaviour of the government, the trade unions and the corporations. And these institutions are not portrayed as inhibitions to workings of the market, but as the necessary institutional apparatus by means of which the modern market economy is run.

We have already talked about the role of the government in Chapter 4. Where do trade unions and corporations fit in?

The role of trade unions

The purpose of a trade union is to attempt to achieve higher real wages and better working conditions for its members. Trade unions do this by playing the market game: by organising and disciplining their section of the labour force to attempt to fix the terms on which their particular category of labour is bought and sold. But the organisation of trade unions is not just an aspect of bargaining in the labour market. The mass organisation of labour is a necessary complement to modern factory production. It is virtually impossible to conceive of a sophisticated system of mass production without some form of organisation, acceptable to the workers, through which decisions and agreements can be made covering the broad majority of the industrial labour force, decisions not only on pay and hours, but also on the detailed organisation of work. The less representative trade unions are, the less effective they will be. If trade unions did not exist, then, in a modern industrial economy, they would have to be invented.

The role of corporations

The same may be said of the modern corporation. The modern large corporation is essentially a financial organisation that switches

masses of finance, which it either owns or can borrow, between alternative lines of production, attempting to maximise the profits it earns on its investments. In a tough competitive world, corporations are continually changing what they produce, how they produce and where they produce, seeking out competitive advantage. The modern corporation, large though it may be, is no less competitive than the nineteenth-century firm, but competition operates in a rather different way. Price competition is now of less importance than product competition. Instead of always changing prices to fit the requirements of the market place, firms concentrate on the discovery of new lines and new processes. Indeed it is difficult to imagine a modern industrial economy in which price competition played a predominant role. If prices fluctuated according to the day-to-day vagaries of the market it would be virtually impossible to carry out the detailed cost-and-revenue calculations essential to large-scale production.

So prices are predominantly simply mark-ups on costs. Competition takes the form of keeping ahead of the game by means of continuous change of product and process. The modern corporation, an institution designed for change, is the institutional embodiment of competition.

An 'institutional' theory of inflation

The institutions which characterise labour markets and product markets, the trade unions and the corporations, define the way the market economy works. In particular, the development of bargaining procedures has institutionalised the labour market. That market now operates through the formal machinery of collective bargaining. Together with modern corporate management of mark-up pricing collective bargaining procedures amount to an attempt to index-link wages and profits. This means that both sides of the labour market are attempting to strike a bargain which preserves or enhances the real spending power they receive. But since they must do this by striking bargains in terms of pounds, shillings and pence – the trade union negotiator does not ask the employer for extra meat and vegetables, plus an extra shirt, plus one more pair of children's shoes – and by fixing prices (and these are two separate operations) there is no reason to suppose that either side will obtain the outcom they expect or hope for.

If workers see real wages falling as prices or taxes rise, the

demand higher money wages in order to redress the balance and, indeed, in order to keep real wages rising at the rate to which they have become accustomed over the years. Corporations maintain their profitability by putting up prices as costs rise. Now if the economy is growing steadily and output per worker is rising, increases in money wages do not affect costs too much and prices are raised less rapidly than wages. The spending power of wages increases and so do profits, a relatively harmonious situation. But if output stagnates or even declines, the struggle of workers to raise wages eats into the normal profits of companies who promptly raise their prices, hence cutting the real value of wages. In reaction, the unions demand the wage increases they need to restore their position to what it was before the price rise. This raises costs, and so prices, and so wages again, and so on and on, in an upward merry-go-round. Nor does it need a decline in output as such to set this process off. A wage cut from an external source, such as a rise in the price of imported oil or big tax increases, will set it going. This is just what happened in the early seventies.

The merry-go-round will continue to spin while the demands of the unions, the companies and the government on the national product add up to more than the product. It can be stopped either by increasing the product to satisfy all demands, or by persuading or forcing one section of the community to reduce its demand. Since the war incomes policies in Britain seem to have played just this role. The diagram shows the real take-home values of wage settlements since 1949 – allowing, that is, for changes in prices and taxes. A striking characteristic of the series is the steady trend increase in real wage settlements which seems to have been built into the fabric of collective bargaining in Britain, a trend which gave real increases of about one per cent per year. Equally striking is the fact that deviations from the trend may be clearly associated with periods in which incomes policies were in force, only to return to trend when the policy was abandoned or broke down. The current situation with its unprecedented levels of unemployment has introduced a new element into the story, using unemployment to force real wage settlements way below trend, storing up, perhaps, a future money wage explosion.

So, according to this 'institutional' view of inflation, the increases in wages and prices are simply the result of dispute over the division of the spoils in a market system, a dispute which will be exacerbated when output is growing slowly or not at all. It is nobody's fault,

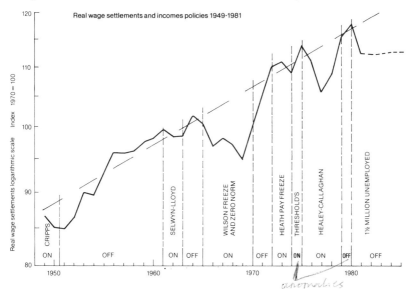

The real wage settlement index is taken from the pioneering work of Roger Tarling and Frank Wilkinson. The index measures the real value to the workers of the wage levels agreed at national bargains, making due allowance for changes in prices, taxes and national insurance contributions. On the relationship between real wage settlements and incomes policies, Tarling and Wilkinson write:

> Postwar incomes policies have all been associated with a real value of wage settlements below what appears to be the normal negotiating level for national bargaining. This normal level shows an upward trend of just under 1 per cent per year ...
>
> ... The Stafford Cripps incomes policy following the 1947 devaluation of sterling had an immediate effect in depressing settlements but quickly broke down as import prices rose following the devaluation and the commodity price explosion of the Korean War boom. The recovery of real wage settlements from 1950 to 1955 was achieved with rates of increase of money wages at around 7 per cent per year. Between 1955 and 1961, real wages at settlement increased at the 'trend' rate, while money wage increases halved to between 3 and 4 per cent per year. The Wilson incomes policy from 1965 to 1969 pushed real wage settlements over 10 per cent below trend by 1969. The collapse of the incomes policy was rapid and money wage increases rose from below 5 per cent per year to about 13 per cent per year in 1970 and 1971. The Heath incomes policy had little impact because of its threshold clause. The various stages of the Social Contract between 1975 and 1978 brought the real wage at settlement down to 7 per cent below trend in 1977, and money wage increases fell below 10 per cent per year. After the collapse of the

policy, real wages at settlement regained their trend level by 1979 and money wage increases rose to 16 per cent per year. (*Cambridge Economic Policy Review*, 1980, no. 1, p. 26).

Two other excellent articles by Tarling and Wilkinson, which provide empirical evidence for the 'institutional' theory of wages outlined in the text, are 'The social contract: post-war incomes policies and their inflationary impact', in the *Cambridge Journal of Economics*, 1977, and 'The movement of real wages and the development of collective bargaining in the U.K.: 1855-1920', in *Contributions to Political Economy*, 1982.

neither the trade unions', nor the corporations'. It is simply the way in which conflict and disruption manifest themselves in a market economy. It can be stopped either by removing the source of conflict or by forcing one of the protagonists to back down. The costs of the latter strategy may be very high.

The 'institutional' view in different countries

An institutional theory of this type cannot be expected to identify relationships which hold across countries. Different countries will have different institutional arrangements for the fixing of money wages, and even where the institutions are formally similar they will have their own peculiar histories which affect the way in which the bargaining parties react to any given situation. There is in Germany a well-known fear of inflation, ingrained by the dreadful experience of the inter-war hyper-inflation in which the currency was destroyed and with it German democracy. In other countries, such as Italy and Japan, there is a greater acceptance of steady inflation, and bargaining and price-setting procedures are adapted accordingly. In some countries high inflation may break out only when output ceases to grow. In others, inflation is a means of mitigating the disruptions of rapid growth. In all, stagnation will tend to accelerate inflation. Though the institutional theory cannot, by its very nature, guide cross-country comparisons, its adherents do claim that they can interpret the experience over time of inflation in any one country.

Inflation theory and inflation policy

So now we have two entirely different theories of inflation, based on different views of the operation of the market system. And the answer given to our earlier question – symptoms or disease? – is different in the two cases. For the monetarist, inflation is a disease inflicted on the healthy body of a market economy by the power of vested interests, private and public, or, perhaps, by the sheer folly or weakness of governments. The institutional theorists, on the other hand, see inflation as a symptom of failings elsewhere in the economic system, a necessary corollary of any economic change in which a large section of the community loses out. Perhaps not surprisingly, the two theories point to diametrically opposed policy conclusions.

As we have seen, the monetarists see the market as ensuring full employment and the supply of money as determining the rate of inflation. Inflation can be reduced by cutting government spending, weakening the trade unions and removing any other inhibitions to the operations of the market.

The institutional theory sees inflation as the outcome of the *inability* of the market to ensure full employment and steady growth. Inflation can be cut by increasing government spending to stimulate the economy and increase employment and output so that the various demands of workers, corporations and government can be met. The supply of money has no major role to play. The government should therefore concentrate on stabilising interest rates to reduce the cost of borrowing to industry.

Is inflation a Bad Thing?

But neither of the theories of inflation I have outlined has brought us any nearer to an answer to the initial question posed in this chapter: Is inflation the Bad Thing that we have all been taught to believe it to be?

Clearly, in a period in which money wages and money prices are rising, some sections of the community may suffer, namely those who are unable to keep up with the game. Anyone whose income is fixed in money terms will fall into this category. And in recent years prices have risen more rapidly than take-home pay, but this was not so much a product of inflation, as a product of slow growth. In normal times, by the very definition of inflation, most prices and wages are going up, so the losses are confined to relatively small groups.

The crucial issue is: Does inflation really damage economic performance? If we compare the experience of different countries the

Table 4. Index of consumer prices   Index 1970 = 100

	UK	US	W. Germany	France	Italy	Japan
1950	44.8	61.7	64.5	38.6	50.6	38.7
1960	67.2	76.2	76.9	67.3	67.9	57.2
1970	100	100	100	100	100	100
(1975)	184.4	138.6	134.7	152.8	171.1	172.4
1980	362.2	212.3	164.7	250.4	375.1	237.6

Inflation rates (percentages)

	UK	US	W. Germany	France	Italy	Japan
1950-60	4.1	2.1	1.8	5.7	3.0	4.0
1960-70	3.9	2.6	2.6	4.0	4.0	5.7
1970-80	13.7	7.8	5.1	9.6	14.1	9.0

Source: OECD *Main Economic Indicators*

Note: The acceleration of inflation in Britain above the rate of Japan takes place mostly after 1975.

answer is clearly no. Until recently the rate of inflation in Japan was higher than in Britain, and the rate of growth of output much higher. On the other hand, both Germany and the United States had very low rates of inflation, and while Germany has had a very high rate of growth of income per head, the United States is the only major country to have a rate of growth of income per head as slow as that of Britain. Nor does inflation necessarily result in a country's products being priced out of world markets. Italy and Japan both had relatively high rates of inflation in the sixties and seventies, and both increased their shares of world industrial markets. The United States had a low rate of inflation, and its share fell dramatically.

Indeed inflation *can* bring some benefits. The seventies saw an increase in the rate of inflation in all the major industrial countries. Once again there was no obvious correlation between inflation and economic performance. But a significant effect of the general inflation was that the impact of the increased cost of oil on living standards was not as great as might have been expected. For instance, the number of minutes that a British manual worker must work to earn a gallon of four-star petrol has not increased significantly between 1971 and 1980. On an international scale, inflation has been a device for shifting the real burden of the oil price rise between countries, primarily from the industrialised countries on to the Third World.

It is clear that inflation can be a tremendous nuisance to the financial sector of a market economy. Contracts and loans are typically fixed in money terms, and if inflation is high, or accelerates beyond expectations, the lender, often the banker, loses out. And the borrower, often the industrialist, gains. So inflation may encourage industrial investment by cutting the cost of borrowing. But in countries in which the financial sector plays an important role in economic and political life, opposition to inflation is likely to be high. Moreover, if the financial community sees inflation as the major economic evil which may afflict a country, it is likely to react adversely to the pursuit of government policies which it regards as inflationary. Given the central role of finance in a market economy these reactions may inflict considerable real damage. For example, if because of the fear of inflation financiers decide to withdraw money from the economy and invest overseas, they could precipitate a foreign exchange crisis which has nothing to do with the underlying position of the economy. Fear of inflation may have more dangerous consequences than inflation itself.

Inflation is clearly a nuisance, sometimes a terrible nuisance, in that you never know from one week to another how much your pay packet will buy, and continuous renegotiations of wages and prices take up time far better spent on other things. Sometimes, an acceleration of inflation by distorting monetary calculation can result in real losses. But the hyper-inflations in which monetary systems have been destroyed have not been associated with the normal workings of the institutions of a market economy. They have, rather, followed the collapse of political authority, or been associated with appalling foreign exchange problems, such as those created by German reparations, which effectively rob the state of its financial authority. In normal times, inflation is, in general, not a fundamental constraint on the performance of the economy. On the other hand, a balance-of-payments deficit *is*. For a balance-of-payments deficit is a debt to someone else that must be paid. It has been the balance-of-payments crises of the past three decades that have been the true crises in the body economic of Britain.

7

A Tale of Trade and Industry

Since the war British industry has suffered a series of defeats in world markets for manufactures. But the national commitment to free trade has not faltered. Britain's experience stands in sharp contrast to that of France, Germany and, most strikingly, Japan. In all these countries trade policy was an integral part of successful industrial reconstruction; the power of the market was far more tightly constrained than in Britain. Britain is now a declining region of the world economy.

*   *   *

Friedrich List regarded the British devotion to free trade as part of an intellectual and political conspiracy to maintain world economic dominance. If the British failed in this endeavour, any other industrial country that achieved economic dominance would, he predicted, espouse free trade as the only 'rational' and 'natural' system for the organisation of world trade.

In this prediction List has been proved to be absolutely right.

Despite the argument of Cordell Hull, American Secretary of State in 1944, that 'for me unhampered trade dovetailed with peace', it cannot be regarded as entirely due to international benevolence that the United States, previously the most protectionist of countries, became the champion of free trade at the end of the Second World War. It was a fundamental tenet of United States policy that America needed to expand exports to avoid a post-war slump. This required access to foreign markets. So all the barriers to trade which had been erected round the world in the inter-war period had to be dismantled. A primary target was the system of Imperial Preference, set up within the British Empire in the thirties and seen by the Americans as a potential threat to the establishment of a world free-trading system. At the end of the war even the free-trading British were somewhat reluctant to rush too rapidly towards an uncontrolled trading and financial system. All trade and international financial transactions had been strictly controlled during the war, and the weakness of the economy in 1945 clearly demanded that controls be continued. But the Americans now made it a condition of their support for Britain's precarious financial position that free trade and free convertibility – that is, the absence of any controls on the exchange of pounds for dollars – should be restored as soon as possible.

List's argument was confirmed yet again in 1981. Since the war Japan has pursued, by formal and informal means, a strict protectionist policy – until, that is, the last decade or so, in which formal import restrictions have been considerably relaxed. By 1981 the competitive strength of Japanese manufacturing industry was such that, in June of that year, Prime Minister Suzuki could afford to argue that free trade was an essential component of a rational world economic system.

The British commitment to free trade

Where List has been proved totally wrong is in his belief that Britain would abandon her eager advocacy of free trade once she was no longer economic top-dog and the rationale for the policy had gone. List, perhaps, had too conspiratorial a view of economic policy. What he failed to appreciate was the potential for intellectual and institutional inertia built into the free-trade programme.

The period of nineteenth-century economic success, the golden era of British free trade, established a leading role in British economic and political life for a number of institutions and social groups whose interests are international and whose continued prosperity is more closely linked to the maintenance of free international economic relations than to the prosperity of the home economy. Both the financial community and the larger industrial companies have this international perspective. For them the ability to move money round the world, to invest wherever the likely return

is greatest, is a basic requirement. So their advocacy of free trade has
survived the decline of British manufacturing at home. It has,
moreover, successfully overwhelmed any anti-free trade arguments
which, coming from those sections of industry and labour hard hit
by foreign competition, have typically been dismissed as the special
pleading of vested interests, the bleating of those who have failed.

But probably of equally great importance to the success of the free-
trade argument has been the intellectual inertia which has afflicted
thinking on economic policy. Modern economics was created in
nineteenth-century Britain, and, not surprisingly, it then reflected
the economic concerns and prejudices of the day. What is more
surprising is that it continues to reflect those prejudices today.
Although subject to more elaborate qualification than might have
been the case eighty years ago, the doctrine that free trade is an ideal
survives. It is enshrined in the mathematical theorems of the
economic theorists, and from there it has been transplanted into the
thinking of those who regard themselves as essentially practical.

The practical case for free trade is that it brings with it the
bracing wind of competition and the urge towards specialisation
which are the very stuff of economic efficiency. The more
competitive producers will drive out the inefficient and those who
refuse to shake up their ideas. The large markets of a free-trading
world will encourage large-scale production and bring forth the
technological advantages of international specialisation.

What the practical case neglects is where the efficient producers
will be, and where specialisation will take place. What if all the
efficient producers happen to be foreigners and all the specialisation
takes place abroad? What benefit then for the home economy?
Appeal to the economists' argument will not help. For the
economists' case for free-trade is developed in terms which eliminate
all relevant considerations by assumption. It is assumed that the
economy is always at full employment and that the balance of
payments always balances: the market mechanism takes care of
that. And it is assumed that capital is not internationally mobile.
Nor, it is less unreasonably assumed, is labour.

It is difficult to think of a set of assumptions with less relevance to
the experience of Britain since the war. The practical person's view
of competition has been all too well confirmed, to Britain's
detriment. As restrictions on trade were dismantled during the
fifties, it became more and more evident that British manufacturing
was unable to sustain its competitive position. The economy entered

a vicious circle of cumulative decline in which an uncompetitive manufacturing sector faced a low, or even falling, rate of growth of demand, with the consequent cuts in investment and productivity growth reinforcing the lack of competitiveness. The whole process was reflected in a perpetually weak balance-of-payments position, puncturing even the weakest growth balloons with the sharp needle of a balance-of-payment crisis.

The final outcome has been the de-industrialisation of Britain. By this frightening term is meant not the disappearance of manufacturing industry as an activity, though this has indeed begun to happen in the last five years or so, but rather the deterioration of the competitiveness of manufacturing to such a state that the manufacturing sector is unable to sustain its position on world markets and is therefore unable to defend the balance-of-payments position at any reasonable level of employment. It is in this international context that the decline of Britain must be assessed. For it is in the international context that we shall find the millstones between which the British economy has been ground.

Is manufacturing really necessary?

But before proceeding to examine these millstones we must face the question: Why all this fuss about manufacturing? Cannot the British turn their hands to other activities to which they may be better suited?

Part of the answer to these questions has already been given in Chapter 3. All evidence points to growth of manufacturing industry as being the key determinant of the growth of the economy as a whole. An expanding manufacturing sector spreads its dynamism through agriculture, distribution and services. Manufacturing is the key to the modernisation of the economy.

In the international context this answer has an added piquancy. If the manufacturing sector is allowed to decline and Britain imports more manufactures as well as her usual quota of food and raw materials, what is to be sold to pay for these imports? Wherein does Britain's comparative advantage lie? Britain cannot become a net exporter of agricultural goods or raw materials, and oil exports will only last for a few more years.

The most obvious area in which Britain seems to have some advantage is in services. The banking and commercial sector, including insurance and shipping, though challenged by the development of financial services in New York, still seems capable of holding its own in the world. But holding its own is not good enough if it is to become the mainstay of Britain's balance of payments. For even today exports of manufactures earn twice as much revenue as do all private services put together. So a 10 per cent fall in manufactured exports would have to be balanced by a 20 per cent increase in exports of services. Even though the overall competitive position of services has not deteriorated over the last ten years (which means that they have performed a good deal better than manufacturing), it is difficult to see where such a massive improvement might come from. Our undoubted comparative advantage in teaching English as a foreign language would not seem to offer much hope.

So manufacturing it must be. And the explanation of why the decline of British manufacturing which began at the end of the nineteenth century should have continued since the Second World War is crucial to our understanding of what has happened to Britain.

Trade and industry since the war

It might have been expected that at the end of the war Britain would recapture the virtuous circle of growing demand and productivity growth that had been lost seventy years earlier. British industry was worn out after five years' intensive production with little replacement or modernisation. But most of Britain's main competitors had been decimated in the war, and there was a tremendous demand for industrial goods throughout the world as reconstruction got underway. British engineering factories could have their pick of customers. In 1950 Britain held a 27 per cent share in the world trade in metal and engineering goods, a marked improvement over the 20 per cent of 1937 (though not so impressive when set against a share in 1899 of 39 per cent). But this share was already beginning to fall yet again. By 1954 it was down to 24 per cent, all the loss being to West Germany. Somehow Britain had missed the boat.

Why Britain failed to jump on to a virtuous circle of cumulative causation is a complex question, but a number of factors are clear, and behind almost all of them looms the balance of payments.

A first major element in Britain's failure was the reaction of both Labour and Conservative governments to the balance of payments problems and international financial difficulties which assailed Britain after the war. Whenever something went wrong with the balance of payments, domestic investment was hit on the head.

Britain had ended the war with a combination of enormous debts, sharply reduced exports, and a buoyant demand for manufactured imports, particularly from America. All this placed an enormous strain on the overall balance of payments. There was a desperate need to export. Demand for British exports was high, but there was a major shortage of capacity. To boost exports every machine that could be sold abroad should be sold, to the detriment of new investment in Britain, and to the benefit of her competitors setting up new plants.

In a White Paper on the 'capital cuts' published in 1947, the Chancellor of the Exchequer, Sir Stafford Cripps, argued that 'As the credits granted by the United States and Canada are now almost exhausted, a great effort to balance overseas payments is necessary', and more resources for exports 'can only be obtained to any significant extent by postponement of certain investment projects. The size, scope and number of these projects must therefore be reduced ... to save scarce labour and materials for diversion to even more urgent ones.' Similarly, in 1949 the government argued that in the following year ' ... investment at home in engineering products should be slightly less than in 1949, and that the products so released and the whole increment in output in 1950 should be exported'. In 1952 further steps were taken to cut investment. And despite some concern about low levels of investment, the balance-of-payments crisis of 1955 brought another exhortation from the Chancellor, R.A. Butler: 'Business firms should endeavour to slow down investment not of the greatest national urgency.'

The successive government restrictions on investment had their effect. By 1950, after five years of reconstruction, total investment in Britain, including investment both in machinery and in building, was only 12 per cent of gross national product. In France it had reached 14 per cent, and in Germany 18 per cent.

A second factor, which has a significant bearing on the rate of recovery of Britain's competitors, is that the amount of industrial capacity destroyed in Germany and in France was not as great as is commonly supposed. The United States Strategic Bombing Survey, which was charged with assessing the economic impact of wartime

Table 5. Gross domestic fixed capital formation as a proportion of gross domestic product, 1950-1980

	UK	US	W. Germany	France	Italy	Japan
1950	12	19	18	14	—	—
1960	17	17	25	19	23	24
1970	21	17	26	23	21	35
1980	18	16	24	21	18	32

Sources: R. Nurske, *Review of Economics and Statistics*, 1956
OECD *National Account*

Gross domestic fixed capital formation measures the output of machines and other durable means of production, residential construction and other construction. It is a measure of the resources society devotes to investment.

bombing, found in 1945 that about 80 per cent of Germany's industrial capacity was still intact. All that was needed was the appropriate organisational framework to get the system going again and the foreign exchange to provide necessary materials. The former was provided for by the reorganisation of the West German government and the German financial system in 1948-9. The latter was provided for, at least in part, by Marshall Aid. Moreover, it should be remembered that at least as important to production as machines is the knowledge and skills of the labour force, including the managers. This had not been lost during the war.

A third factor was Britain's rapid plunge into the icy waters of world competition. The quasi-protected market of the Empire was soon lost, though not the high level of military expenditure that went with it. In 1948 the Labour government staged a 'bonfire of controls'. Then, in 1951, the new Conservative government was elected with a mandate finally to abolish the remaining controls and restrictions which seemed to characterise the grey post-war years. This did not mean just the burning of ration books. In 1947 all manufactured imports were strictly controlled. By 1955 only 34 per cent of manufactures were subject to import control, by 1958 only 13 per cent. Restrictions on the convertibility of sterling were also eased, with full convertibility being restored in 1958. So, although the economy would never again be as open as it was in the halcyon days of nineteenth-century free trade, by the end of the 1950s Britain had effectively returned to her traditional free-trading stance.

And we never had it so good.

In a booming world economy, fuelled by American foreign expenditure, Britain grew as fast as at any time in her entire history as an industrial nation. But Britain was growing significantly more slowly than the rest. The weaker economy was living on the economic crumbs from the tables of the strong.

Stop-go

This was the era of stop-go – of recurrent balance-of-payments crises, each more severe than the one before. The response to each crisis made sure of that.

The reaction of successive governments to balance-of-payments crises was to deflate the economy by tax increases and restrictions on credit, and by limiting the spending power of wage earners by means of incomes policies. The old policy of discouraging investment at times of balance-of-payments crises was also continued. The overall strategy undoubtedly worked. Imports were cut, and some sort of balance was restored to the balance of payments. When balance was restored, the economy was boosted again, usually by the politically popular expedient of cutting personal taxes to encourage consumption.

This procedure, instead of alleviating the trade and payments difficulties faced by Britain after the war – out-of-date capacity, loss of empire, huge debts – added further difficulties by eroding the competitive position of British manufacturing. The slow-down in demand and in investment reduced the rate of productivity growth. Therefore, when the economy was reflated, British industry was less competitive than it had been before the crisis, imports rose more rapidly than before and so precipitated the next crisis. The policy designed to correct the immediate balance-of-payments problem helped create the longer-term deterioration of the balance-of-payments position.

Of vital importance, however, were not so much the fluctuations in demand, the stops and the goes, as the low general rate of growth of demand. Britain's balance-of-payments position could not sustain an average rate of growth demand as great as that enjoyed by her competitors. In particular, the rate of growth of demand for manufactures was significantly lower in Britain than in other major industrial countries.

De-industrialisation

By the end of the fifties the die was cast. Although investment had grown with the world boom and with the aid of tax allowances designed to encourage industrial investment, the share of investment in national income was, by 1960, still significantly lower than in West Germany, Italy and Japan, and was to remain so through the sixties and seventies. Productivity growth had also been lower than in all major industrial countries other than the United States. The vicious cycle of cumulative causation was firmly entrenched. Attempts by the Labour government to escape foundered in the foreign-exchange crisis of 1966, as did the Conservative government's attempt to expand out of the vicious cycle in the early seventies. But even as late as 1974 the scale of the problem was not so great as to precipitate large-scale unemployment. In that year there were 550,000 unemployed. By 1976, however, the balance-of-payments situation was so bad that the government was forced to succumb to the deflationary dictates of the IMF. The short march toward three million unemployed had begun.

In the 1950s the relative decline of the manufacturing sector, though it proceeded apace, made little impact, for manufactured imports took such a small part of the home market for manufactures. In 1955 only about 5 per cent of the entire market was taken up by imports. So, even if imports grew rapidly, they did not make too much of a dent on overall home production. But they grew and grew, and at the same time the export performance of British manufacturing deteriorated. As the share of imports in the home market rose to 26 per cent in 1980, Britain's overall share in the world trade in manufactures shrank from 18.5 per cent in 1954 to less than 7 per cent in 1980. After 1975, import penetration could not even be warded off by a self-induced slump; imports kept rising.

The vicious circle of cumulative causation has slowly ground down the competitive position of British manufacturing. In recent years the impact of this decline on the balance of payments has been partially masked by the bounty of North Sea oil. None the less manufacturing competitiveness, or lack of it, is such today that without the cushion of oil, the balance of payments would be in deficit to the tune of about 5,000 million pounds, even though there are more than three million unemployed who are less able to afford the imports that they would buy if they had a job. To put it another way, without oil there would have to be about two million more people unemployed if the balance of payments were to balance. To put it yet another way, if current trends continue in the next year or two Britain will import more manufactures than she exports for the first time since the sixteenth century.

How did our competitors do so much better?

Priorities in economic policy

A common characteristic of economic policy in France, Germany and Japan, was the clearly perceived link between industrial policy and international trade policy, a link which the British, in the grip of the Keynesian Ideology, appear to have failed completely to notice.

British economists and politicians were seduced by the excitement and grandeur of economic policies which attempt to manage the economy at an overall level. Keynesian theory seemed to provide the answer to the failings of the market economy. Now the government could take responsibility for the management of total demand by manipulating taxes and government spending. It might not be possible to choose a level of demand which could both achieve full employment and a suitable rate of inflation or balance-of-payments position, but these too should be tackled by overall national policies. The rate of inflation could be tackled by some deflation and the application of incomes policies. And the balance-of-payments problem could be solved by deflation and devaluation.

By contrast industrial policy was something for detailed, tedious, even nit-picking administration – often in the less attractive regions of the country, and apparently having little to do with the grand economic design. The link between industrial policy and international trade was tenuous and, to the extent that it existed at all, once again primarily an exercise in mollifying the particular industry hard hit by foreign competition, smoothing its orderly demise.

In the nineteenth century free trade *was* an industrial policy. The opening up of world markets, and the easy import of raw materials and food was clearly in the best interests of British manufacturing. But even when it had outlived its usefulness as an industrial policy, free trade was retained and the problems of domestic industry placed low in the national order of priorities. Concern about the fortunes of manufacturing has not been totally absent, of course. Investment allowances have become steadily more generous since the war, and the National Economic Development Office was set up in 1962 to conduct detailed research into industrial problems. But the various schemes emanating from these initiatives have not amounted to a new trade and industry policy.

The priorities of Britain's competitors could not have been more different.

In all her major competitors, with the now customary exception of the United States, industrial policy stood at the very centre of economic policy. Industrial policy was the key to the reconstruction of a competitive industrial sector which would secure the trading position of the nation. General overall management of the economy should deal with short-run fluctuations in the balance of payments or inflationary pressures, but it should not interfere with medium- and long-term industrial programmes. The brunt of any necessary short-term fluctuations in demand should be borne elsewhere. In France, for example, despite repeated use of monetary policies in an attempt to contain inflationary pressures, the authorities consistently took steps to ensure that medium-term credits of which they approved were not affected by the credit squeeze. Similarly, the German banks were committed to the medium-term financing of industry, a commitment that was not to be shaken by short-run ups-and-downs in the economy as a whole.

But stable financial provision, though important, was not enough. A key component of an active industrial policy had to be an active trade policy, ensuring that fluctuations in international markets, or foreign competition in the home market, did not interfere with the progressive development of manufacturing industry.

French policy

France's trade policy was quite different from Britain's. In place of the hectic rush towards free trade in the fifties, trade in the French economy was tightly controlled. In 1960 the proportion of manufactured imports to gross domestic product was the lowest in Western Europe. Only in the early sixties did the regulations of the newly formed Common Market enforce the dismantling of tariffs and other formal barriers. And even since then the French have never shown themselves unwilling to bend the rules of the Market whenever they think it in their best interests – while they have, of

course, preserved their protectionist stance towards countries
outside the Common Market. To the British visitor a notable feature
of Parisian streets is the absence of Japanese cars.

Moreover the role of protection was not just to protect, but also to
guide. The use of protection was an integral part of the industrial
policies of the *Commissariat Général du Plan* in the fifties. Variations in
the rate of protection were important as both carrot and stick in
directing the policies of French firms. But the crucial role played by
protection was that it permitted the formulation and execution of
long-term investment plans, public and private, which were not
abandoned in the face of short-run fluctuations in international
markets.

The German experience

France has a long tradition of centralised direction of industry and
trade which provided the institutional, and intellectual, context for
the formulation of post-war economic policy. The situation in
Germany was nominally completely different. Odious comparisons
with fascism created a revulsion against the centralised management
of economic affairs. Past traditions must be abandoned, and there
must be a commitment to economic liberalism – domestic laissez
faire and free trade – as the counterpoint to the development of
political democracy.

But reality did not fully fit the new appearance. The Federal
Government operated a wide variety of discriminatory subsidies and
tax concessions designed to develop domestic manufacturing –
especially heavy industry – and to encourage exports. Subsidies,
when manipulated appropriately, can be every bit as successful a
protective device as tariffs. Andrew Shonfield calculated that in
1961-2 German discriminatory subsidies to all branches of the
economy amounted to £963 million pounds, £276 million of which
was directed toward trade and industry. In the same year British
subsidy payments amounted to £617 million, most of which was
devoted to agriculture and only £74 million of which went to industry
and trade.

German industrialisation was also aided by massive investment in
the basic public framework for industrial production – roads,
railways, power and water supplies, and so on. These investment
programmes did not fluctuate in the face of short-run variations in
economic conditions and so provided a stable home demand for the

products of German heavy industry.

Subsidies and public investment therefore provided the environment in which the consensus of industry, government and the banks could guide the reconstruction of German industry – a reconstruction which was consciously directed toward success in trade in manufactures.

The great Japanese experiment

While Britain's European neighbours pursued industrial policies based on quite different economic philosophies and, indeed, quite different economic institutions from those prevalent in Britain, the most dramatic use of trade policy as a means of industrial reconstruction was necessarily found in the country which, at the end of the war, was the most backward: Japan. In 1950 income per head in Japan was less than a quarter of the level per head in Britain, and less than a sixth of the level in the United States. Japanese industry was technologically backward, and production was concentrated in slow-growing lines – cotton textiles made up a quarter of all exports. Moreover Japan is notably deficient in natural resources. Although home production can supply about three-quarters of food requirements, the country must import about 90 per cent of all energy requirements together with virtually all basic ores. The Japanese economy could only grow by means of manufactured exports. And that is just what happened. Japan's share of world trade in manufactures grew from less than 4 per cent in the early fifties to 15 per cent in 1980 – a gain which is approximately equal to the sum of the losses of Britain and the United States. The value of Japanese exports of manufactures exceeded that of Britain's in the late sixties, and will soon exceed the value of American manufactured exports, making Japan the second largest exporter of manufactures, West Germany being the largest.

The great debate

Back in 1949, how Japan was to escape from its industrial backwardness was a matter of great debate. The traditional economists' view was put forward by the Governor of the Bank of Japan, Mr Ichimada, who argued on automobile production that 'since Japan should develop its foreign trade on the basis of the international division of labour, efforts to develop the automobile industry will be futile'. The Ministry of International Trade and Industry took a quite different view: 'since the development of the automobile industry to a high level will lead to the modernisation of the machinery industry, and, consequently, all other industries, it is desirable to concentrate all possible efforts on raising its productivity and international competitiveness so that it can catch up with other advanced countries.' MITI won the argument, not just for automobiles, but in establishing its philosophy of trade and industrialisation as the foundation stone on which Japanese economic policy would be erected.

This policy was to be focussed on a clear objective – the development of a manufacturing industry which would be sufficiently competitive to enable Japan to sell enough abroad to purchase the raw materials and fuel which she totally lacks. And the means were clear too, embodied in the powers of MITI itself and expressed in economic policies designed to protect manufacturing from foreign competition, to allow it to grow in the context of the domestic market and then to export on the strength of a sound home base.

Trade policy and the industrial development strategy

The first priority in the industrialisation programme was to select those industries which were to be the object of conscious development and those which were to be left to fend for themselves. Japan's traditional, and at the time major, exports such as low quality textiles and toys were to be left to fend for themselves. Development policies were to be directed toward the new industries, iron and steel, modern synthetic textiles, electronics, industrial machinery and automobiles.

The industries which were selected for development were then the object of a two-pronged policy linking trade and industrial development.

First, they were protected from foreign competition by a comprehensive range of controls – tariffs, excise duties designed, for example, to give an advantage to Japanese automobiles, controls on foreign investment and foreign exchange control. Foreign exchange control meant that only a limited amount of dollars could be allotted to the purchase of automobiles – no more was available and so, when it was used up, no more foreign automobiles could be imported. In 1953 this allocation amounted to $13,740,000, permitting the import of 5,900 cars. In 1954 it was cut to $610,000, permitting the import of 370.

Secondly, MITI controlled the purchase of foreign patents. To develop rapidly, Japan desperately needed foreign technology. Since purchase of patent rights involved a transaction with a foreign country it came under MITI's jurisdiction and could be used as a means of ordering and directing industrial development. In synthetic fibres for example, MITI geared the issue of licences to import foreign technology to the need to maintain a high rate of growth of demand for the petrochemical industry. Licences were also a means of stimulating fierce competition in the home market. In synthetic fibres the issue of licences was staggered. First one firm alone would receive a licence, gaining a virtual monopoly – but with the knowledge that in three or four years another firm would receive a licence. The first firm was, therefore, forced to develop as rapidly as possible. It could not abuse its monopoly position. And firms had to earn their right to a licence by proving to MITI that they were the most go-ahead firm around.

The role of the home market

The trade and industry strategy worked. Firms grew rapidly on the basis of home demand. From 1955 to 1961 the production of passenger cars grew from 50,000 to 250,000, but still only 11,500 were exported. Indeed the proportion of exports in the total output of firms in the licenced industries, i.e. the new developing industries, actually fell throughout the sixties as production rose. And within the rapidly expanding, though protected, home market, the growing firms competed vigorously in design, quality and price.

It was not until the mid-sixties that Japanese industry became competitive in world market terms. The 50,000 passenger cars produced in 1955 had cost $2\frac{1}{2}$ times as much as equivalent European models. In 1980 Japan produced three million passenger cars. And although they were not necessarily cheap, they outcompeted foreign vehicles in just those non-price aspects – engineering design, reliability, delivery, servicing – which are central to modern industrial competition.

Although trade policy was the key manipulative instrument in the pursuit of industrial development, it was supplemented by an active internal policy of subsidies and state 'guidance'. This has become particularly noticeable in the second phase of Japanese industrialisation which is proceeding today. A new policy is being pursued in which Japan will move on from the growth industries of the sixties and seventies, such as televisions and automobiles, to new 'knowledge-intensive' scientific industries. This move is being facilitated by heavily subsidised research programmes. The key characteristic of the new industries is not only that they produce products for which demand is expected to grow rapidly, but also that they use a very small proportion of imported inputs in the value of output produced. They are another way of cutting imports.

So the central component of Japanese industrial policy has been the use of the home market and trade policy to secure the benefits of the virtuous circle of industrial growth. Growth of home demand encourages investment and productivity growth. Then products are launched on foreign markets. Even today Japan is predominantly a home-market oriented economy, with manufactured exports accounting for only 9 per cent of total domestic production, a figure barely changed from 1960 and in stark contrast to Britain's 18 per cent.

Table 6. Manufactured imports and exports as a proportion of gross domestic product, 1960 and 1978

	UK	US	W. Germany	France	Italy	Japan
1960 Imports	4.8	1.3	4.0	6.3	5.5	2.1
Exports	12.9	2.6	8.3	14.1	7.8	8.3
1978 Imports	15.3	4.9	9.7	10.5	9.7	2.0
Exports	17.8	4.6	11.7	16.5	17.9	9.3

Source: IMF *International Financial Statistics*

While all this was going on in Japan Britain relied on the market to arrange trade and industrial affairs in a suitable manner. The steady erosion of Britain's share in world markets for manufactures was masked by the high rate of growth of world trade which provided a soporific cushion on which Britain's economists and politicians could rest – just as the high flow of dividends and profits earned from earlier investments had eased Britain's decline at the end of the nineteenth century. But the air was leaking from the cushion.

An unintentional trade and industry policy for Britain

There has been one important period in Britain's economic history, however, when, in the face of *force majeure*, the commitment to free trade and the market has weakened. This was in the 1930s. The collapse of world trade in the depression forced all countries to turn inward. Britain was no exception. The return to gold in 1925 had placed a heavy foreign burden on domestic economic policy, deflation and high interest rates being necessary to maintain the value of sterling. In 1931 the fateful enterprise was at last abandoned. Britain left the Gold Standard for good and sterling was devalued. In the same year a variety of tariffs of up to 100 per cent were imposed under emergency legislation, culminating in 1932 in the Import Duties Act which imposed a general 10 per cent tariff. The Ottawa Conference of 1932 set up the system of Imperial Preference, which, in Britain's case, involved raising tariffs yet further on foreign goods rather than cutting tariffs on Empire products.

Now the foreign market no longer dictated domestic policy. Freed from their role of supporting sterling, interest rates were cut to 2 per cent. Cheap money precipitated a building boom. Demand rose for just those industries which had previously suffered most from French, German and American competition – electronics, chemicals and automobiles. British industry underwent a more rapid modernisation in this period than at any other time in its history. The results can be seen around many towns in the south-east and the Midlands: arterial roads lined by 1930s factories, like the magnificent Hoover factory at Perivale, surrounded by 1930s suburban villas. The export branches – coal, shipbuilding and steel – were hopelessly depressed, and kept the overall rate of unemployment miserably high. But the new industries were flourishing in the home market.

This process of modernisation slowed during the war – though of course production was directly war-oriented and the interests of manufacturing industry had top priority. In the 1950s the gains were to be squandered.

The Hoover factory ceased production in 1981.

Lessons

What lessons can be drawn from the experiences of Britain's major competitors and of Britain herself in the thirties?

The first is that, in a world in which the market for manufactures is intensely competitive, there can be no satisfactory industrial policy without a related trade policy. The international market will overwhelm domestic efforts which ignore this fundamental rule. The options open to any one country depend on its ability, if necessary, to insulate its manufacturing industry from the rigours of the world market. This means that for small countries the options are rather narrow, and they must hitch themselves to a larger waggon. But for a country the size of Britain the available options are certainly wide enough to accommodate any reasonable industrial policy, as the 'accidental' policy of the thirties illustrates.

A second lesson is that, if domestic manufacturing is to prosper, both the financial community and large corporations must have a national orientation. Unfortunately, the successes of the nineteenth century left Britain with just the opposite, an outward-looking financial system and large companies that were accustomed to organising their affairs on a world scale.

Thirdly, since industrial policy requires a trade policy, and trade policies involve detailed economic administration by the state, successful industrial policies have required a high degree of government involvement in the running of the economy. The market is given far less scope. Government involvement has not been linked to political parties of any particular hue. It has rather been linked to recognition of the need to manage the market.

Finally, the experiences of Japan, and to a lesser extent of France, point to what can be done by means of decisive policy backed by suitable powers in a propitious economic environment. Unfortunately we cannot expect the same results to be achieved by Britain today. The rapid growth of the Western world in the fifties and sixties contributed greatly to French and Japanese success. In the tougher climate of the eighties things will be more difficult. These difficulties, however, make the need for decisive policies greater rather than less.

This then is the tale of trade and industry in Britain today: a declining region of the world economy – in Nicholas Kaldor's chilling phrase, 'the Northern Ireland of Europe' – a country relying on the market to solve problems which the market only reinforces, encumbered not merely by outdated institutions and vested interests but by irrelevant ideas. All social and political energies seem to be devoted to attacks on some of the symptoms of decline – inflation and trade union militancy – while ignoring the true disease, the cumulative decline of manufacturing industry created by the market.

8

A Good Servant, but a Bad Master

The prospects facing the British economy are bleak. A recovery programme geared to the attainment and maintenance of full employment will encounter difficulties from balance-of-payments problems, the fear of inflation, social and economic inertia and the need to formulate a suitable industrial policy. These problems can be overcome, but the solutions pose major social and political questions for Britain.

*　*　*

Being British is going to be even less fun in the future. The economic prospects are bleak. Some people will undoubtedly have a good time, even enjoy a little prosperity, but the bitterness of decline will seep around them. The next decade may be punctuated by occasional upswings and desperate U-turns to and fro, but these will founder as the vicious circle of cumulative causation grinds on. That, at least, is how it looks from the perspective of the winter of 1981-82.

In all the confusion it is difficult to spot the fundamentals of what is going on. It is so easy to misread symptoms, for the market economy is not a mechanism that readily reveals its inner workings. Economists have been struggling for two hundred years to penetrate its appearances – the behaviour of firms, of workers and trades unions, of money markets and international markets – to examine the substance beneath. They have not come up with any agreed solution. What they have come up with is a wide range of hypotheses and conjectures which, with a little rough handling but not enough violence to bend the truth unrecognisably, I have classified in two broad groups – on the one hand theories claiming that, at its best, the market is an automatic mechanism which ensures an efficient allocation and use of resources, and, on the other, those theories denying that the market amounts to such a beneficent mechanism. It will be evident from what has been said above that I myself regard the latter theories as those which are appropriate to a constructive analysis of Britain's problems.

Rejection of the idea that the market is an automatic mechanism ensuring full employment does not involve rejection of the view that the market is an engine of dynamic change. That would be silly, considering what the market has done since 1776. There is a powerful impulse in a market economy towards accumulation and innovation – competition sees to that. The principle of cumulative causation which has played a central role in my argument has been constructed out of the ideas of the writers who applauded that impulse, Smith and Ricardo, and out of those of Keynes, who recognised that the growth of demand, on which the impulse depends for success, is not automatically forthcoming. Indeed the competitive struggle which powers growth and change can be perverted into a mechanism of decline and stagnation. Like fire, the market is a good servant, but a bad master.

How then, should we interpret the experience of the West in the past three decades, and what lessons can be learned for the future – the future of Britain, in particular?

Lessons of post-war experience

The period since the war has been a time of rapid growth and spectacular change. The countries which have done relatively poorly out of this, Britain and the United States, are those that have relied predominantly on the market to take them through. Those countries which have, one way or another, attempted to manipulate the structure of their economies in favour of industrial development and in which economic development was conceived in a longer-term perspective – France, Germany and Japan – have done best. But manipulation is not enough. The economy can only respond if plans for industry are combined with a high rate of growth of demand. No amount of planning will make an economy dynamic in a slump.

French planning was a miserable failure in the inter-war years. Here we have the fundamental problem facing the West. How can we ensure, within the context of the existing international arrangements, that all countries can maintain a rate of growth of demand for manufactures that will return them to a reasonable level of prosperity? It appears highly likely that we cannot. The deflationary bias of the international monetary and trading system seems sure to condemn the West to, at best, a period of economic confusion – the final outcome of which is impossible to discern.

What then can be done with Britain in the hard days ahead? I do not intend to present an economic blueprint for Britain's recovery. Such a blueprint would necessarily involve a wide range of social and political issues which are outside the scope of this book. Moreover such a blueprint would inevitably be too heavily infected with my own prejudices to be of interest to most readers. Instead I shall try to sketch the broad economic parameters of a viable recovery programme. However the ends are to be achieved, these are the issues that must be faced; and, as far as I can see, this is the type of approach that must be adopted.

Full employment

The primary objective of any recovery programme must be a return to full employment. By this I mean a return to the situation which prevailed until the early seventies, with unemployment oscillating between 350,000 and 500,000. This will not be easy to do, for in recent years the deterioration of the economy has proceeded to such a degree that any rapid increase in employment will be checked by bottlenecks, shortages of machinery and shortages of skills that will take some time to make up. The return to full employment will take a number of years, but it should none the less be the ultimate end in view.

In social terms, making full employment the primary objective of the recovery programme requires no justification. But even for the hard-headed economist it has an overwhelming rationale.

First, unemployment is a straightfoward waste of resources. If full employment were restored, annual production would be greater than it is today. That increment of production is now being lost for ever.

Secondly, the presence of large-scale unemployment indicates that the growth rate of output is lower than it might have been. In Britain, as in all industrial countries, the low overall growth rate is attributable to the low rate of growth of demand for manufactured goods and the consequent loss of the benefits of cumulative causation. A higher growth rate of demand will not only serve to eliminate unemployment in the longer run, but will also enrich the economy with a faster rate of technical progress and hence with greater competitiveness. In a tough, competitive world these gains will be necessary if full employment is to be maintained. Without them, the loss of competitiveness will set the wheels of cumulative causation working in reverse. Decline will be inevitable, and full employment unattainable.

It may be argued that, even if demand were to grow at the highest feasible rate, the rate of productivity growth in Britain would still be insufficient to establish an economy capable of competing on equal terms with other Western countries. This may conceivably be so – though why exactly the British should possess some inherent inability to compete it is difficult to say – the weather perhaps? But even if it is so, a full employment, highest *possible* growth strategy, is still the only reasonable objective of a recovery programme. The inherent lack of competitiveness will simply imply that steps must be taken to insulate the economy from the harmful effects of foreign competition.

Is full employment possible?

The objective of full employment is not, however, uncontroversial.

The current recession has awakened in some quarters a peculiar fatalism which suggests that a return to full employment is impossible, even undesirable. On the one hand some argue that modern technological developments, the development of microelectronics and so forth, will enforce unemployment in the future. Workers will simply not be required. The striking thing about this widespread argument – which, by the way, was also popular in the thirties – is that there is no evidence for it whatsoever. If microelectronics were precipitating a dramatic fall in the demand for labour, this fall would be reflected in dramatic increases in output per worker in the more advanced industrial countries. But this has not happened. Believers in technological unemployment have confused the effect of technical change on the demand for labour in one particular trade with its effect on the economy as a whole. The confusion has a long economic history, going back to early nineteenth-century debates on the effects of the introduction of machinery.

A different case for the inevitability, and even desirability, of unemployment has been made on the grounds that more production, more growth, will destroy the environment and exhaust the supplies of many materials necessary for the maintenance even of current levels of well-being. There is no doubt whatever that much of the work involved in manufacturing industry is unpleasant and even dangerous, and that industrialisation despoils natural beauty. But those who argue for a halt to economic growth on these grounds have failed both to notice that economic growth is directly linked to improvements in general standards of living – to cuts in infant mortality, for example – and to distinguish between the form which growth takes today and the form it might take if it were more rationally organised. How society might best decide what is to be produced is again a topic beyond the scope of this little book; but as far as leisure is concerned, it should be clear that this ought to be a product of technical progress demanding less effort, rather than of unemployment rejecting the efforts that are available.

Again, the argument that resources are going to run out is a hoary one. Jevons, for instance, argued in the 1870s that Britain could not grow faster because she would rapidly run out of coal. But it is of considerable importance. Of course the exploitation of the world's resources should be better organised, but this should not disguise the fact that Britain's current decline, and indeed the problems of the West as a whole, are independent of the problem of resources. It is true that a rational solution to the exploitation of resources is not likely to be found through the market – the recurrent chaos in the world market for oil is evidence enough of that – but this is an insufficient reason for abandoning the attempt to solve the economic problems that can be solved. Moreover the technological innovations which will overcome the constraints which limited resources place on economic development are unlikely to be forthcoming in a slump. The current recession, for example, has encouraged complacency about oil supplies and led to a slow-down in energy-saving research and development.

So the arguments of the pessimists should be rejected. Full employment must be the objective.

A policy for full employment

What policies are required to set the economy back on the road to full employment? The economists who believe in the self-adjusting efficiency of the market mechanism would look to the market and to policies which enhance its power. But on both theoretical and empirical grounds this prescription is profoundly mistaken. As we have seen, the theory of the automatically adjusting market contains major logical deficiencies, the practical significance of which has been confirmed by events of the past decade. None the less many policy makers have been led by this theory to confuse the efficiency which the competitive market imposes on the individual firm, with the efficient operation of the economy as a whole. All the firms in the economy may be operating with commendable efficiency, or at least doing the best they can, in an economy with high levels of unemployment and social waste. The running of the economy cannot be equated with the running of a grocer's shop.

Monetarism is the most bizarre form taken by devotion to the market, for as well as relying on a mechanism that does not work, cuts in government expenditure, designed to lower the growth of the money supply, reduce demand and worsen unemployment.

As the market cannot ensure full employment, the government must step in to maintain a sufficiently high rate of growth of demand. In current circumstances, the growth of private expenditure on consumption and investment is bound to be somewhat limited, and, as will be further outlined below, growth of exports cannot be relied upon. So the state will have to take responsibility for at least the initial steps in the recovery programme. Increasing the level and rate of growth of demand will involve higher government expenditure and lower taxation. Higher expenditure may take the form of direct government investment programmes on roads, railways and hospitals, and in the nationalised industries. Reduced taxation should stimulate greater expenditure by private consumers and investors.

This will result in the government's running a larger deficit, though the increase in the deficit will be somewhat offset by the reduction in dole and other welfare expenses as the number of unemployed is cut. The larger deficit will require greater government borrowing. However, higher incomes imply higher savings and the government should have no difficulty in following the sensible strategy of arranging its financial affairs round an interest-rate target rather than a monetary target.

But even though a sustained growth of demand is a necessary condition for a revitalisation of the British economy, we cannot be certain that it will prove sufficient to do the trick. All the evidence from our successful competitors points to the need to organise and direct the development of manufacturing industry and to ensure that there is an adequate flow of finance to keep the wheels of industry well-oiled. Moreover the huge scale and complex organisation of modern production requires that both finance and demand should be stable and sure in the medium and the longer term.

So there's the answer. To break out of the vicious circle of cumulative causation and set a virtuous circle in motion, a high and steady rate of growth of demand for British manufactures backed by a suitable industrial policy is required. What is stopping us?

The balance-of-payments constraint

Well, a number of things. But, above all, the fundamental constraint on the maintenance of the necessary rate of growth of demand is the likely consequence for the balance of payments. Any attempt to return to full employment now would, despite the cushion of oil exports, result in an unsustainable balance-of-payments deficit as the newly employed bought their share of French, German and Japanese goods. So much of the extra demand simply flows overseas.

An export-led recovery?

The increase in imports could only be sustained if exports expanded rapidly too. Indeed it would be an ideal situation if the increase in demand came from increased exports. But without a dramatic improvement in British competitiveness (only attainable *by* an increase in demand) greater exports could only come from a major expansion of the world economy leading to greater imports by Britain's trading partners. If the rest of the world were to embark on a new expansion, Britain's problem would be eased, though not solved.

Unfortunately Britain cannot expect any help from this direction. Quite the reverse. The deflationary bias of the world trading system is likely to assert itself with renewed vigour in the next decade as the continued relative decline of the United States further erodes the remaining vestiges of central organisation and the policies of the IMF reinforce, rather than ameliorate, the downward pressure. The economic problems of the United States pose the biggest threat to the future prosperity of the West. For not only have they robbed the system of its most powerful Big Spender, but the deteriorating competitive position of American industry is likely to force deflationary policies on the U.S. government, giving a violent deflationary twist to the world economy. The United States buys nearly 12 per cent of all the world's manufactured exports, and any cut in American demand has major ramifications round the world, particularly in the weaker countries like Britain.

So, in the absence of any radical new international initiative, the international trading system is likely to be a major source of instability. Countries which are heavily exposed to the vagaries of the international market, like Britain and West Germany, will suffer most, though of course Germany is better equipped to weather the storms. Even the less exposed countries, such as France and Japan, may well be forced to trim their policies to the international wind. The brave attempt of President Mitterand's government to expand out of the recession is likely to founder on the rocks of a balance-of-payments deficit, and even the Japanese would suffer in a major world recession. Already some German bankers are discussing the possibility of the formation of a new *Zollverein*, a customs union within which the more powerful Common Market countries could be insulated from the world market and from which Japanese goods would be excluded. If things reach such a desperate pass even a little exposure would be a dangerous thing.

So Britain cannot rely on the relief of a sustained expansion of the world economy. There may be some improvement if the price of oil does not rise too much, inflicting new deficits on the West, but the system will still be terribly unstable. Moreover, even if there were a sustained world expansion, this would be insufficient to improve the *relative* competitiveness of Britain. Indeed the situation might well be made worse as others grab greater shares of the expanding market.

Britain must, therefore, look to the home market to provide the necessary growth of demand for manufactures. Not only is the home market more readily controlled, but home demand constitutes by far the greater proportion of demand for the products of each industry. Typically 80 per cent of manufactured output is absorbed by the home market. But if demand is to grow by expansion at home, Britain must fashion her own solution to the balance-of-payments problem which stands in the way of prosperity. For a rapid expansion of home demand will suck in more imports, whatever happens in the rest of the world.

Whatever happened to the oil boom?

Cannot North Sea oil foot the bill? The discovery and exploitation of large oil reserves in the North Sea seemed to herald a new chance of prosperity for Britain. Not only would the burden of expensive oil imports be lifted, but oil revenues might be used to finance an expansion of the economy – that is, to cover the balance-of-payments deficit which would otherwise follow from the expansion. But this has not happened. North Sea oil now contributes about £7,000 million to the balance of payments, but the decline of manufacturing continues apace. Has oil proved to be a curse in disguise?

The idea that oil might prove to be a curse derives from the history of the Dutch Disease. This is not something which afflicts elm trees; it is the affliction of large energy exports, in this case of natural gas, on the economy of the Netherlands. The Dutch economy was, in the late fifties, one of the most dynamic in Europe, with a fast-growing, highly competitive manufacturing sector. Growing exports of natural gas, however (in the latter half of the sixties), forced up the value of the Dutch guilder, steadily undermining the competitiveness of manufactured exports. Exports of manufactures were replaced by exports of gas, and the resulting unemployed received benefits paid for out of gas revenues. The eighties find the Netherlands with declining gas revenues, stagnant manufacturing and high unemployment. This is a stark example of the way in which the market handles the blessing of natural wealth.

A contraction in manufacturing industry like that suffered by the Dutch, is not, however, the 'inevitable' outcome of the temporary bounty of oil. Oil revenues can, and should, be used to sustain the rate of growth of demand for domestic manufactures rather than replace it. This is particularly true for a relatively weak country, like Britain, for whom oil revenues can provide a breathing space within which to expand. The Dutch problem was that gas revenues were allowed to strengthen an already strong balance-of-payments position, and the Dutch were content to sit back and live on the proceeds. This is not Britain's problem, though an occasional rise in the exchange rate brought about by swings of speculative finance may make it appear so. For Britain the oil revenues have loosened the noose of the balance of payments a little – just think how terrible the situation would be without them – but not enough. They have not provided a sufficient cushion to permit a rate of expansion fast enough to ensure a return to full employment – only sufficient, perhaps, to obscure the true severity of the problem.

Since oil has not produced a magical solution to Britain's problem out of the North Sea hat, any proposal to deal with Britain's economic problems must say how it intends to deal with the balance-of-payments problem. Three options are available.

Deflation

Deflation will balance payments in the foreign exchange markets, but it will only reinforce the vicious cycle of cumulative causation which already has Britain in its grip. It is the negation of what is needed.

Devaluation

Devaluation may help to make British goods more attractive at home and abroad, but the use of devaluation as a strategy for long-run expansion can only be regarded with scepticism. Not only are cheaper, but inferior, British goods unlikely to command a greatly expanded market; but any benefits of the devaluation will rapidly disappear in the consequent inflation. Wages will be bid up to recover the loss in purchasing power suffered in the devaluation, for since the object of the entire exercise is that the economy should be expanded, there will no longer be three million unemployed to keep wages down. Devaluation may be a part of a satisfactory recovery programme. But it is incapable alone of loosening the stultifying grip of balance-of-payments deficits. Large devaluations will create more problems than they solve.

Planned trade

There is only one alternative trade policy left – planned trade. This means imposing a set of regulations, be they tariffs, or exchange controls, or quantitative restrictions, which prevent the purchase of foreign manufactures as the economy is expanded. Demand will be turned inward towards British manufactures. The level of protection can be varied in such a way that a full-employment rate of growth of demand is sustained.

Direct action of this kind on the current account should be supplemented by policies on the capital account designed to stimulate the growth of domestic manufacturing, or at least to eliminate financial outflows which place an unnecessary burden on the overall balance of payments. The abolition of exchange controls in 1979 resulted in a massive outflow of capital as the main institutional investors – insurance companies and pension funds – bought foreign securities. In the following financial year net investment by these institutions in Britain was *nil!* An outflow of this magnitude, amounting to more than £2,800 million, imposes a great burden on the balance of payments. More must be exported, or less imported, to cover the bill. All capital exports should be strictly assessed, and permitted only if they meet the criterion of contributing to the expansion of British industry, either directly, or indirectly by loosening the balance-of-payments constraint.

Objections to a protective policy

What are the objections to such a policy? Apart from the misgivings of those who believe that the market knows best and should not be interfered with, there are four major objections to a protection strategy.

First, it may be argued that a policy of protection would be a reversal of the movement towards more open economies which was an essential component of the post-war boom. It would invite retaliation by Britain's trading partners which would negate any advantages by cutting British exports. And it would push the Western system down the slippery slope towards the autarchic chaos of the 1930s, when country after country desperately cut imports and world trade had, by 1934, fallen to less than half its 1928 level.

This argument may well be correct in the prediction that Britain's trading partners would retaliate, but it fails to recognise that such retaliation would be peculiarly irrational. For Britain operates already, without inciting retaliation, a powerful form of protection which is successfully cutting imports. It is called unemployment.

The proposal is not to use protection to cut imports further, but to substitute protection for unemployment as a means of keeping imports to a level which can be afforded. In other words, imports should not be cut. To cut imports and run a surplus, so imposing a deficit on someone else, would be a beggar-my-neighbour policy. Rather, imports should not be allowed to increase as demand is raised back to full-employment levels. If Britain's trading partners still insist on retaliating, even though as a whole they will be selling as much as ever (some countries may on balance be losers, and others may gain), negotiated trade quotas will be the only answer. And in such negotiations Britain would have a strong hand to play – in a reciprocal exercise of retaliatory import cuts between Britain and Japan, for example, Japan has far more to lose than Britain. There is, however, no reason why things should come to such an aggressive conclusion, if the content of the policy is clearly spelt out. Britain's expansionary national policy would be in the best interests of the international system. Indeed, if only trade could be planned on an international scale, a similar rational solution for the West as a whole would be on the cards.

A second, related, argument against the protection policy is that it would be contrary to so many of Britain's international treaty obligations, including the obligations undertaken on joining the Common Market. This is not the place for legal arguments, even if I were competent to make them, which I am not. But it is not really a legal question. The point is whether it may be agreed that Britain is a more valuable member of the Common Market, and indeed of the Western community of nations, if she is prosperous or if she is in economic decline. Since the answer is obvious, the debate should be on the means of achieving prosperity, not on formal rules which are irrelevant to the end in view.

A third argument against using protection as part of the recovery programme is that it will be used to featherbed defunct, out-of-date industries that should be closed down. This is clearly a danger. If the workers in such industries would otherwise join the ranks of the long-term unemployed, feather-bedding is not a bad thing. But it clearly has no role to play in the dynamic economy envisaged by our recovery programme. The object of protection is not to keep defunct industries going, but to permit the maintenance of the high level and rate of growth of demand which will facilitate the closure of defunct firms. One of the dangers of Britain's current situation is that protection will be introduced in a piecemeal fashion precisely to prop-up declining firms, rather than as part of a general recovery programme.

A fourth objection is that the protection policy will be used to reduce the prospects of Third World exporters gaining access to the British market, so that Britain's prosperity will be purchased at the expense of the poorer countries of the world. In a rationally organised world trading system this would not happen, for a rational system would discriminate only against surplus countries, and Third World countries are notoriously deficit countries. Britain cannot organise a rational world system on her own, and British import controls might reduce imports from some Third World countries. But such countries are more likely to benefit from an expanding, modern British economy than from a depressed Britain introducing piecemeal protection for her old-fashioned industries which cannot compete with the Third World.

So, all in all, the objections to the use of protection in the recovery programme do not carry much weight – particularly when it is noticed that any policy leading to balanced international payments will involve similar ends achieved by far less constructive means.

There are, however, other major inhibitions to the implementation of the recovery programme: the fear of inflation, the possibility that even if demand is expanded output will not respond, and the possibility that even if output does respond the response will not be conducive to sustained expansion.

The fear of inflation

The greatest immediate danger to the recovery programme is that the policy of protection (and perhaps a little devaluation) combined with a high rate of growth of demand for manufactures will collapse in an explosion of inflation. The upward spiral of inflation will be given a powerful twist by a combination of factors, which are all essential components of the programme.

Protection will mean that home consumers and producers will be forced to buy British goods that they would prefer not to buy. These might not be more expensive, but they will tend to be uncompetitive in one way or another. This will be particularly important in the case of machines, for costs of production will be increased and prices pushed up. Prices of imported goods will also tend to rise, both because of shortages and because tariffs may be levied on them. The overall effect can be mitigated by tax cuts paid for from tariff revenue, but price rises in some industries are inevitable.

But of far more importance is the fact that the expansion of demand in the circumstances of an economy such as Britain today is likely to lead to an increase in inflation, independently of any effects of the protection policy. As we saw in Chapter 6, real wages have in recent years fallen far below their usual trend levels, and if history is anything to go by, once the fear of mass unemployment is removed there will be a rapid increase in money wages as workers attempt to recover the real spending power they have lost. The increase in money wages will not have the impact on prices that it would today because the higher level of demand will produce a higher level of output and so there will be more to go round. But it will be some time before output has risen enough to set wages back on trend.

A possible reaction to the inflation problem is to do nothing and simply weather the inflationary storm in the confident hope that productivity growth will eventually solve the problem. The fear of inflation, however, has become so deeply ingrained, particularly in the financial community, that a wait-and-see strategy may bring the whole programme into disrepute, leading ultimately to a general loss of confidence and financial collapse. The alternative is an incomes policy which limits money wage increases and also, like incomes policies in the past, limits the rate of increase of real wages. Given the record of incomes policies in cutting real wage growth, there is no doubt that the imposition of any incomes policy would be strongly resisted. The problem is essentially political. Incomes policies and fears of inflation have, in the past, been used as part of a political programme to shift the cost of (typically) cutting demand for imports on to the real incomes of wage earners. Once the political content of any anti-inflation policy is clearly recognised and acknowledged by all, the way is open to make a reasonable deal.

Inflation will be given a further twist by the fact that the expansion of demand will inevitably lead to an increase in the overall liquidity of the economy. The expansion of demand by the government will result in a larger budget deficit which, if there is any prospect of damaging increases in interest rates, should be financed by means of the sale of liquid government assets. This, in turn, will increase the liquidity of the banks, who will be dripping with money to lend. In so far as the available money is spent on industrial goods, it will be a useful component of the expansionary programme. But past experience has shown that part of the increase in available credit will be used in the housing market and in land speculation, sparking off a boom in house and land prices. These unwanted consequences can only be limited by direct inhibitions on the issue of credit, and then only with the active cooperation of the financial community. Indeed the support of the financial community, or at least the absence of its active hostility, is a necessary part of the entire programme. For financial speculation, particularly across the foreign exchanges, could easily wreck the whole enterprise before it has even begun.

A moribund economy?

Serious doubts about the viability of a recovery programme arise from the concern that the rate of productivity growth will not respond in the manner that the principle of cumulative causation would predict. The drive toward modernisation may be halted by deep-set deficiencies in the organisation of British manufacturing industry, such as trade-union hostility to innovation, and the lack of dynamic leadership said to characterise British management, deficiencies that the recovery programme could reinforce. In the protected expanding home market, the power of the trade unions will be enhanced, and firms will be prepared to settle for a quiet life when the pressure from overseas competitors is relaxed.

The problem of industrial relations is extraordinarily complex, constructed as it is out of years of bargains, tactical manoeuvres, betrayals and famous victories. Industrial relations do not, however, exist in a vacuum. The institutions on each side of the bargain are the vehicles through which a market economy works, and thus through which the process of cumulative causation will, at least in part, be manifest. Both trade unions and modern corporations are essential components of the modern industrial economy, antagonistic though they may, on occasion, appear. They are necessary to facilitate large-scale production, to stabilise conflict and order change. In a relatively prosperous economy the mutual organisation which they bring to the market system helps overcome some of its perfidious uncertainty.

But in a declining economy these same institutions can become perverse agents of self-destruction. Trade unions, in a desperate attempt to preserve the jobs of their members, resist technological advances which would throw people out of work. Corporations don't invest when the prospect of profit has disappeared, worsening the situation by cutting demand and productivity growth. Moreover a corporation can leave the sinking ship and invest and produce abroad. The cumulative forces of the market economy find reinforcement in the institutions through which the market works.

After a period of decline as long as that suffered by Britain, the institutional inertia will be very great, and it cannot be expected that industrial relations will change overnight. Old habits die hard. Improved industrial relations can always be imposed with the bludgeon of unemployment, but the cost to the economy is high, both in reduced investment and in increased resentment. Indeed the 'cure' of unemployment exacerbates the underlying disease by cutting true productivity growth associated with modernisation, in favour of the degenerate productivity growth of fewer workers operating out-of-date machines. However, a growing demand for products and for labour will inevitably facilitate a more favourable environment. Workers will be more willing to participate in the introduction of new techniques if this clearly does not mean higher unemployment and does mean larger wage packets. Equally, employers will be prepared to provide workers with more solid prospects of continuing employment if they are confident of buoyant markets. The famous enthusiasm of Japanese workers for technological change has more than a little to do with the guarantees of employment provided by their employers.

The possibility that British companies will simply sit back and enjoy the easy prosperity of a protected home market also poses a threat to the reconstruction programme. How to tackle this problem, if problem it be, is a matter for industrial policy, on which I shall have more to say in a moment. Suffice it to say at this point that without the growing market afforded by the protection policy, companies would have neither the means nor the incentive to modernise anyway.

An industrial policy

The expansion of demand in a protected economy, necessary though it is, may well not prove sufficient to set the economy off on a virtuous circle of cumulative expansion. The strategy of limiting imports of manufactures is not, of course, merely a device for cutting the overall value of imports and so loosening the balance-of-payments constraint on growth. It is also intended to direct demand specifically toward the manufacturing sector. But the experience of our competitors suggests that even this directed increase in demand will not be enough to reverse past trends. A more detailed industrial policy is required.

Here we can learn from our competitors. The bases of a successful industrial policy are control of demand, control of finance, and some direct influence on investment and hence on the evolution of the structure of industry. Control of demand can be achieved via the government's spending and taxing decisions, including spending on subsidies, and by control over imports. Finance and methods of direct influence pose more complicated problems.

The experience of France, Germany and Japan since the war teaches us that a successful reconstruction policy requires some system of central direction and coordination, and in market economies this means some form of direction of flows of finance.

Finance

A peculiar characteristic of the British financial system is the relatively small role that the banks play in the finance of industrial investment. The mirror image of this is that British companies finance about 80 per cent of their investments out of retained profits, rather than by borrowing. So, paradoxically, the sophisticated financial mechanisms of the City of London are of little help to the problems of British industry. Indeed some of those institutions may be positively harmful. The day-to-day fluctuations of the value of company shares on the Stock Exchange, for example, encourage a concern with short-run ephemera to the detriment of the long run, and so to the detriment of investment and growth. In the financial systems of our competitors, stock exchanges play a much smaller role and have far less influence.

The British banks and other financial institutions have often been criticised for their evident unwillingness to provide long-term finance to industry. But it should be remembered that the provision of such finance would require a complete revision of the relationship between finance and industry. The arm's-length relationship which typifies the British scene will not do when long-term financial risk is at stake. Yet a reconstruction programme for the British economy will require the injection of long-term finance into manufacturing industry on an unprecedented scale. An institutional reform of the financial system is required comparable to that undertaken in Germany in the 1870s. What the precise content of such a reform might be is not of great importance. But it would be surprising if something resembling the French or German system of industrial banking were not to be adopted, with a complementary reform in the organisation of corporate management and finance and a larger role for the state as ultimate guarantor of risky ventures. The crucial point is that the interests of the financial community should be subjugated to the interests of manufacturing industry.

A role for the market

A suitable financial mechanism would give policy makers another important lever on industrial development. But in Britain's highly concentrated economy other stimuli may well be required to prevent firms from simply taking advantage of their newly protected situation by earning monopoly profits. In this the market can play an important role. In the same way in which MITI has deliberately stimulated competition between firms attempting to win licences to import technology or access to foreign exchange, so the British government could force firms to compete to 'win' finance or access to limited imports. This will only work if the government is willing to be ruthless and discriminate actively in favour of the successful company; even to see the unsuccessful go to the wall. For, paradoxically, a successful industrial policy has almost as much to do with closing down lines of production as opening new ones. In a depressed economy closing down production involves a total loss and exacerbates decline. In the context of a growing, fully employed economy such changes are part and parcel of innovation and growth.

Direct influence

The policies pursued by the successful industrial countries suggest that demand growth and financial provision must be coupled with more detailed intervention in the evolution of the structure of industry. Simply throwing money at firms will not do. After all, the British government has been doing that for years. The level of investment subsidies and tax allowances to industrial companies in Britain is already so high that *net* taxes on corporate profits are extremely low, on average about 7 per cent.

The problem to be tackled is how to direct investment toward the future. This involves the formulation of the broad lines that the evolution of the economy will take, and the direction of firms toward goals which they can as yet but dimly perceive and hence are reluctant to rush towards. The immediate, short-term calculation of profit and loss must be replaced by a longer-run perspective. This Japanese-style approach will lead to some mistakes being made. The Japanese investment in plastics, for example, proved a costly error, particularly when confronted by the rapid rise in the price of the basic raw material, oil. But the costs of these mistakes are unlikely to approach the losses in real income which derive from the misdirection of investment and innovation by the market left to itself. What is needed is that competitive drive inherent in a market system should be reawakened and harnessed to the recovery programme by providing new constraints and new stimuli which guide the individual firm within a coherent general policy.

Institutions

These are the broad outlines of the type of programme that might reverse Britain's decline and set the economy off on a virtuous circle. The institutional form that the programme might take is a matter for debate. After all, the institutions of France, Germany and Japan are very different from one another: in France a protected, highly controlled economy, in Germany an open economy in which a system of economic consensus is mediated through the banks, in Japan, now more open too, domestic competition of an intensity unknown to the West is combined with long-term industrial planning.

In Britain the institutions must be devised to launch the three-pronged attack of a high rate of growth of demand for manufactures, direct controls on the balance of payments and a discriminatory industrial and financial policy. This programme seems obvious enough when viewed in the light of the experience of other major Western countries. In the British context, however, it appears positively revolutionary. It involves changing the economic conventions and institutions of a century or more, and accordingly stepping very heavily on a number of sensitive and highly influential toes. None the less there is no reason to suppose, politics apart, that a programme of this type cannot be successfully carried out. After all, it's been done before.

During and immediately after the Second World War the British economy was run as a planned economy, and with a quite remarkable degree of success. All trade was tightly controlled, and allocation of materials, together with government control of demand, was used as a basic method of organising production. The mobilisation of Britain's economic resources was the most efficient of any of the combatants during the war. But with the end of the war the planning mechanism was rapidly dismantled. The controls were not converted into a mechanism for detailed peacetime planning like the Monet plan in France, but instead were reoriented toward purely overall objectives, such as limiting inflation by means of price controls. Even the control of imports, which played a crucial part in the improvement of the balance-of-payments position immediately after the war, was to be rapidly abandoned.

It is true that war implies very special economic and social circumstances – there is a well-defined objective of all policy, a broad social consensus that the objective is desirable, and a willingness to accept restrictions on personal economic choice. The lesson that can be drawn, however, is that *in extremis* the institutions necessary to change and control the economy can be devised, and conscious, detailed policies can be implemented with more than a fair measure of success. When there is a real need, all the blather about monetary policy, the efficiency of the market and the need to cut government spending is immediately forgotten. Instead the emphasis switches to production and the institutions that ensure that production takes place. This lesson has been forgotten or ignored. Instead, the economic destiny of Britain has been handed back to the market, and the calculations of the market place have determined what is best for Britain.

An intellectual revolution?

A reconstruction of the British economy will require, as much as anything, a change in intellectual perspectives and prejudices. It is the economic ideas of the past which need to be overthrown before any straight thinking can be done. The grip of the concept of the efficient market on the minds of economists and practical persons is more powerful than is commonly-suspected. It was, after all, powerful enough to absorb Keynes's assault on the myth of an efficient labour market and to create the far less threatening Keynesian Ideology. And it remains a touchstone even for those economists who, recognising what they conceive of as the imperfections of the real world, reject the simple conclusions of the automatic market theories. As late as 1958 an influential American study concluded that there was little chance of the French economy displaying any real dynamism, for the organisation of the economy was such as to stultify the effect of market forces. At the time France was the fastest-growing economy in Europe. In 1976 a leading industrial economist observed that, despite Japan's economic success, the high level of interference with market forces meant that the Japanese economy was 'allocationally inefficient' – a conclusion that can only draw sighs of relief from the rest of us.

Thinking in terms of our principle of cumulative causation involves some automatic mechanisms too, but the mechanisms are open-ended in the sense that at crucial points in the story, notably the determination of the rate of growth of demand, no automatic forces exist. Instead the particular history of the economy and the institutions it has evolved take a hand. Hence, in this view of economic affairs, the institutions of which any particular economy is composed are not viewed as imperfections but are the very material in terms of which the tale must be told.

Political implications

Despite my avowed intention to avoid the apocalyptic vice of all general economic prescriptions, and to avoid political discussion, the accumulation of argument, bearing one necessary policy reform after another, has culminated in a broad recovery programme which can only be implemented if there is a major shift in the political make-up of Britain. The swing of power, and indeed enthusiasm, back to manufacturing industry, which lost the centre of the political stage a century ago, would be radical enough. But the reorientation of the interests of the financial community and the large multinational corporations back from their worldwide perspective toward the British economy, in which they have for some time taken little interest, would be a reform on the scale of the Reform Bill of 1832.

In the winter of 1981-82, changes do seem to be underway in the political make-up of Britain. But unfortunately the movement appears not to be towards reform, but towards a return to the Keynesian Ideology and the Butskellite policies that have played a considerable role in the creation of the problem.

The stalemate which has characterised British politics since the war is a stalemate with real economic foundations. The interests of labour are in domestic development. The interests of finance and large corporations lie in their worldwide operations. It will be very difficult to break this stalemate and to build a social and political consensus behind a truly viable recovery programme.

Whatever will happen to Britain?

The recovery programme outlined in the broadest terms above is designed to transform the market from a bad master into a good servant. This can only be done if steps are taken to ensure a high and stable rate of growth of demand for British manufacturing industry, which in the world economy today means a high and stable growth of the home market. This apparently simple objective is beset by difficulties both at home and abroad. It will certainly be more difficult to pursue now than it would have been thirty years ago. In the light of these difficulties I cannot help but be pessimistic. If, however, some understanding of how the market system really works were to replace the tattered remnants of the orthodox theory of the automatic, efficient mechanism, there may perhaps be a general change of perspective.

The opposition, intellectual, political, and economic, is powerful and well entrenched. The problems involved in the implementation of the recovery programme are considerable. This is hardly surprising, given the long history of Britain's decline. But the difficulty of the problems pales beside the prospect of doing nothing and leaving it to the market.

The broad lines to follow are clear. It will not be easy.

References

It would be quite inappropriate to clutter a book like this with the paraphernalia of scholarly footnotes and a bibliography. However, an indication both of the books and articles which I have found most helpful in writing the book, and of the further reading available to anyone who wishes to follow up the argument, may prove useful.

The following books provided a substantial part of the background material for the work as a whole:

Eric Hobsbawm, *Industry and Empire*
Charles Kindleberger, *The World in Depression, 1929-1939*
David Landes, *The Unbound Prometheus*
Andrew Shonfield, *Modern Capitalism*

Other references may be grouped under the headings of the chapters to which they are most pertinent:

Chapter 1
Frank Blackaby (ed.), *De-industrialisation*
Angus Maddison, *Economic Growth in the West*
John Kenneth Galbraith, *The Great Crash, 1929*
Joan Robinson, *Economics: An Awkward Corner*
Joan Robinson, *Freedom and Necessity*
Aijt Singh, 'U.K. industry and the world economy: a case of de-industrialisation?', *Cambridge Journal of Economics* (1977)

Chapter 2
John Eatwell and Murray Milgate (eds.), *Keynes's Economics and the Theory of Value and Distribution*
Richard Kahn, *On Re-Reading Keynes*
Joan Robinson, *Economic Philosophy*

Chapter 3
Nicholas Kaldor, 'Causes of the slow rate of economic growth in the United Kingdom', in his *Further Essays on Economic Theory*
Nicholas Kaldor, *Strategic Factors in Economic Development*
Sidney Pollard, *Peaceful Conquest: The Industrialisation of Europe 1760-1970*
Sidney Pollard, *The Development of the British Economy, 1914-1967*

Chapter 4
Frank Blackaby (ed.), *British Economic Policies 1960-1974*
Donald Winch, *Economics and Policy*
Ian Gough, *The Political Economy of the Welfare State*
Donald Moggridge, *British Monetary Policy, 1924-1931*

Chapter 5
Fred Block, *The Origins of International Economic Disorder*
Joan Robinson, 'The new mercantilism' in her *Contributions to Modern Economics*

Chapter 6
Andrew Crockett, *Money*
Nicholas Kaldor, 'Monetarism and UK monetary policy', *Cambridge Journal of Economics* (1980)
R. Sayers, *Modern Banking*
Roger Tarling and Frank Wilkinson, 'The social contract: post-war incomes policies and their inflationary impact', *Cambridge Journal of Economics* (1977)

Chapter 7
J.C.R. Dow, *The Management of the British Economy, 1945-1960*
Ragnar Nurkse, 'The relation between home investment and external balance in the light of British experience, 1945-1955', *Review of Economics and Statistics*
Terutomo Ozawa, *Japan's Technological Challenge to the West, 1950-1974*
Kazuo Sato (ed.), *Industry and Business in Japan*
Sean Glynn and John Oxborrow, *Interwar Britain*

Chapter 8
Books and articles analysing British economic policy abound, but particularly recommended are Nicholas Kaldor's *Essays on Economic Policy*, volumes 1 and 2, and his *Further Essays on Applied Economics*, Terry Barker and Vladimir Brailovsky (eds.), *Oil or Industry?*, Bob Rowthorn's *Capitalism, Conflict and Inflation*, and copies of the quarterly *Cambridge Journal of Economics*, the *Cambridge Economic Policy Review*, and the *National Institute Economic Review*.

Index